YOU DO NOT TALK
ABOUT FIGHT CLUB

YOU DO NOT TALK ABOUT FIGHT CLUB

I AM JACK'S COMPLETELY UNAUTHORIZED ESSAY COLLECTION

EDITED BY READ MERCER SCHUCHARDT

BENBELLA BOOKS, INC.
Dallas, TX

BENBELLA

BenBella Books, Inc.
6440 N. Central Expressway, Suite 503
Dallas, TX 75206
Send feedback to feedback@benbellabooks
www.benbellabooks.com

Printed in the United States of America
10 9 8 7 6 5 4 3 2 1

Library of Congress Cataloging-in-Publication Data

You do not talk about Fight Club : I am Jack's completely unauthorized essay collection / edited by Read Mercer Schuchardt.
    p. cm.
 ISBN 1-933771-52-6
· 1. Palahniuk, Chuck—Criticism and interpretation. 2. Palahniuk, Chuck. Fight Club. I. Schuchardt, Read Mercer.

 PS3566.A4554Z95 2008
 813'.54—dc22

                         2008019337

Proofreading by Stacia Seaman and Yara Abuata
Cover design by Laura Watkins
Cover illustration by Ralph Voltz
Text design and composition by PerfecType, Nashville, TN

Distributed by Independent Publishers Group
To order call (800) 888-4741
www.ipgbook.com

For special sales contact Robyn White at Robyn@benbellabooks.com

CONTENTS

INTRODUCTION

Chuck Palahniuk, Existentialist Paramedic

Read Mercer Schuchardt

Let us say at the outset that, if all great literature is more complex than the naïve reader can suspect, it is equally true that this complexity, once discovered, can be rendered in simple terms.
—Frederick C. Crews, *The Pooh Perplex*

In an early interview with Chuck Palahniuk in *The Onion*,* the following exchange occurs:

O: A lot of *Fight Club's* fans seem to appreciate the movie on a lower level than Kierkegaard might. How do you deal with fans who just see it as a call to anarchy or violence?

CP: Wow. Bummer. I can't control that, you know? All I can control is how much fun it is for me to do it. And beyond

---

*www.theonionavclub.com/avclub3842/avfeature_3842.html

that, I can't control whether people are going to go to it,
whether they're going to like it, how they're going to inter-
pret it. I can't control it, so I don't even worry about it.

O: Is there a wrong way to read your work?

CP: No. I accept the whole Roland Barthes idea of the death of
the author. People are going to bring their own body of
knowledge, their own experience, to whatever. It is possibly going to be, for them, something in contradiction to
what it was for you. I can't control that, so I won't even
worry about it.

The collection you are reading is about that last paragraph. About
readers "bringing their own body of experience, knowledge, and
whatever" to interpreting the cult novel and subsequent cult film
that is still, a decade after the movie and book, the verifiable cult
phenomenon known as *Fight Club*. How verifiable? Well, name
another author whose Web site (www.chuckpalahniuk.net) is called
"The Cult" and whose content gets updated on a weekly, sometimes
daily basis. Oh, and is run entirely by fans, not by the author himself. Or name a living author whose work is still "new" and yet has
already achieved the status of "modern classic" in literary terms, to
the degree that it has inspired two full academic conferences, has
occupied the full issue of a refereed scholarly journal (*Stirrings Still:
The International Journal of Existential Literature*), a documentary
movie, thousands of groupies, and dozens upon dozens of references
in all other areas of popular culture. In truth, whether considering
his novels, his movies, or Chuck Palahniuk himself, the effect of
cult-like devotion is discernible, and that effect begins with *Fight
Club*. *Fight Club* didn't just inspire a movie, it inspired a video game
and a myriad of imitations in manifest cultural forms. From highbrow to lowbrow to nobrow, *Fight Club* is still on the tip of everyone's
tongue. In January 2008 *Fight Club* was the subject of a chapter of
Jonah Goldberg's book *Liberal Fascism*. In May 2006 CNN released a
story* on a real-life fight club in Menlo Park, California, in which it

*www.cnn.com/2006/US/05/29/fight.club.ap/index.html

was reported that "computer techs turn to fisticuffs for fun." Read Palahniuk's own introduction to the tenth anniversary edition of *Fight Club* for an even more extensive list of influences the book has had in the decade since its release. Do an eBay search for "Fight Club" and you'll find more than four hundred items for sale, from signed first editions of the book to the leather jackets and shades worn by Brad Pitt in the movie. With Palahniuk's new novel and the film adaptation of *Choke* both coming out this year, it's safe to say that the Chuck Palahniuk effect is still going as strong as when it first entered into the world as a book in 1996 and as a film in 1999. So while reading what follows, always remember that it "is possibly going to be, for them, something in contradiction to what it was for you."

Put another way, this collection is an attempt to answer the question: Just what is *Fight Club* really about? Is *Fight Club* about "a generation that's had its value system largely informed by advertising culture"?*· Is it a story of male anxiety in a metrosexual world? Of ritual religion in a secular age? Of the genealogy of the doppelgänger figure in world literature? Of the spiritual malaise induced by the technological society? Of the avenues of escape from totalitarian capitalism? Or could it just be a grown-up retelling of the comic strip *Calvin and Hobbes*? Could it be an exposé of Janus mind control programming by government spooks? Is it really a modern version of *The Great Gatsby*, with Jack and Tyler vying for Marla's affections instead of Jay and Tom vying for Daisy—or was it Marla and Jack fighting for *Tyler's* affections? Is it a veiled autobiographical confession of contracting AIDS? Is it a retelling of Pink Floyd's *The Wall*? Of *American Beauty*? Of *The Matrix*? Is the movie a filmed adaptation of *The Unabomber Manifesto*? And what does it have to do with J.R.R. Tolkien, or the myth of Oedipus, or Nietzschean existentialism? No, really: Is it possible that one novel can really be about so many disparate, even contradictory things? Yes, and here's why: As the foremost American novelist with his diagnostic digit on the pulse of contemporary culture, Chuck Palahniuk is a documenter of our

---

*As Edward Norton, discussing his role in the film *Fight Club* at Yale University on October 3rd, 1999, suggested.

world of disparate contradictions. He is our existentialist paramedic: He won't save you, and he won't even give you any medicine, but he'll hold your hand all the way to the hospital. On the way there he'll show you a mirror, let you see just how badly beat up you really are, and in some strange way you will arrive at the ER feeling more hopeful, less lonely, less despairing. He's not religious—not directly—and yet his characters and their stories present the reader with an occasion for something unusual. If confession is good for the soul, whether or not you think you have one, then reading Chuck Palahniuk allows you to admit being you to yourself just a little bit more. And this uncanny knack he has for nailing the zeitgeist, no matter how painful or bizarre it is, is the reason he has any readers, let alone makes bestseller lists. In a world in which no one reads anymore, this is no small feat. Reading Palahniuk is like watching MTV and being reminded of something very important at the same time. *Huh? Go away! Wait, what was that?* You can't fight the sensation that his books give you: that you're rushing right through the really important parts. As he says in *Invisible Monsters*, the novel that technically preceded *Fight Club*: "Well, get used to that feeling. That's how your whole life will feel someday."

No matter who you are, you're going to have to either reach high or stoop low to enjoy the full spectrum contained in this collection. Some authors have Ph.D.s, use very big words (my favorite: *eucatastrophe*) and drop citations like birdseed in their full, scholarly, and academic approaches. Other pieces are more metaphorical, literary, or just display the beautiful and unique snowflake of their interpretation. Some pieces are incredibly short (the shortest: *three paragraphs*), others are incredibly long, but I hope you'll enjoy each one. And while this collection is by no means the complete picture of existing interpretations, you'll find most of the others referenced, quoted, or cited throughout. You'll also notice that this collection, like the Metaphilm Web site (which I cofounded with E.J. Park in 2001 and run to this day with Peter Edman: www.metaphilm.com), incorporates a pretty complete sacred-to-profane spectrum of interpretations. If either end of the spectrum offends you, well then, as Bill Hicks used to say: Forgive me. I don't intend to offend, but when a writer sparks an interest and evokes a response from such a wide array of readers, I think it's worth hearing what they have to say. In fact, Chuck's readership reminds me of two other books whose audiences were wide: Walker Percy's *Lost in the Cosmos*, continuously in print since it was published in 1983 and adored by everyone from *Playboy* magazine to *Christianity Today*, and one of my high school favorites, Frederick Crews's *The Pooh Perplex*, in which the author mimics various academic interpretations of the classic children's book, *Winnie-the-Pooh*, from the perspective of each discipline. Crews's work should perhaps be considered the first to conflate the highbrow academic world with the lowbrow world of popular culture. Its humor stems not only from the satirical nature of the essays, but from the perception one has upon completion that, to a man with a scholarly field, *everything* looks like a blade of grass in that field. While not all of the following pieces are in that vein, you'll find ample opportunity to mutter at each author, "You should get out more often." But then again, you probably go out far too often as it is.

Personally, I've been a fan since the film came out in 1999, and a part-time Chuck Palahniuk follower since I first saw him speak at the Astor Place Barnes & Noble in New York City. I've never seen any author pack a bookstore with a line as long as Chuck Palahniuk has. Standard procedure for his readings is to come three hours early just to get a seat in the *back*. The hardcore fans, they show up—*in costume*—in the morning for a 7:00 PM reading. After *Fight Club*, I've read everything he's written, presented two lectures at the first Chuck Palahniuk conference at the University of Edinboro, and taught his novel *Invisible Monsters* to my Expository Writing students at NYU for three years. I'm told that my teaching of his book was the sole reason that it became *Entertainment Weekly*'s "Cult Book on Campus" for NYU. That could just be hearsay, but I didn't find any other professors teaching it. I know what my students told me: They bought copies for their roommates and discovered that even their mothers were reading it when they went home on break. I read the book seven times before cowriting a screenplay with one of my top students, Adam Karp, who left college in order to go work in Hollywood. Mark Twain once said that he could live six months on a good compliment.

Chuck Palahniuk said of our script: "I loved it. Especially the ending: It made me weep." That compliment lasted me three years.

Since then, Chuck has gone darker with his material while I have tried to go lighter, and my enthusiasm for his work is perhaps best articulated by Flannery O'Connor, who said, "The theologian is interested specifically in the modern novel because there he sees reflected the man of our time, the unbeliever, who is nevertheless grappling in a desperate and usually honest way with intense problems of the spirit." I am no theologian, but Mr. Palahniuk once described himself as a lapsed Catholic, while I would describe myself as a relapsed Anglican. Maybe it's just age, or the effect of having seven children. But I love his work the way I still love Pink Floyd's *The Wall*. It reminds me of a time in my youth, a time that years and wisdom only make glow with a brighter nostalgia. The Bob Dylan thesis explains a lot, too: "I was so much older then, I'm younger than that now." In *Rant*, as in all his novels, Chuck proposes a new (and expectedly absurd) way for humans to find genuine community and transparency with one another. After a particularly gruesome car crash, one character says, "This is how church should feel." I saw a sign in front of a parish in Maine that said: CATHOLICS CAN ALWAYS COME HOME. I don't know if Chuck is heading home or not, but I appreciate the fear and trembling he puts into his work. Like the ghastly skulls—*memento mori*—on the desks of medieval scholars, his gruesome novels nevertheless remind me how fleeting, beautiful, and urgent life is.

On *Fight Club* I have one interpretation printed here, which incorporates some of the insights from three other interpretations, which I've left out for space considerations and in deference to other authors who made similar points and often in a better style. I kept collecting interpretations until it hit me: *This would make a great book.* If you like film analysis, and/or have your own unique interpretation of *Fight Club*, we'd love to see it. If it's good enough, we might even be able to publish it on Metaphilm.

Introductory comments and author bios precede each essay. Many thanks to all our contributors, and especially to Mr. Palahniuk himself for writing the foreword for the collection.

Chuck Palahniuk is the author of the novels *Fight Club, Invisible Monsters, Survivor, Choke, Lullaby, Diary, Haunted, Rant, Snuff,* and the non-fiction collections *Stranger Than Fiction* (which contains "Now I Remember," on the movie *Memento,* first published on Metaphilm) and *Fugitives and Refugees: A Walk in Portland, Oregon* (a travel guide). He lives in the Pacific Northwest. Mr. Palahniuk was gracious enough to write the following piece exclusively for this collection.

FOREWORD

The Fringe Is the Future

Chuck Palahniuk

In Eugene, Oregon, at the University of Oregon campus, near the university bookstore, a row of concrete barricades blocks 13th Avenue. People walking or riding bicycles can enter campus at that point, but cars and trucks must stop. A similar barrier blocks 13th Avenue at the opposite end of campus, leaving the stretch in between as a paved mall for pedestrians, bicyclists, people playing Frisbee-golf. And dogs. When I was a student there in the 1980s, the concrete barricades seemed as if they'd always stood guard.

A decade out of college, I discovered that they had not.

In 1994 the last in a long series of small presses had declined to publish my first manuscript; actually, they'd been declining it so long and so reluctantly that we'd become friends. This small press was run by a married couple, out of the basement of their home in the woods. They'd met each other while students at the University of Oregon in the 1960s, two hippies who'd protested the war in

Vietnam, celebrated the arson fire that destroyed the campus ROTC building, and staged a sit-in to block 13th Avenue.

Back then cars could drive through campus. Some close calls had occurred between vehicles and pedestrians. Some near misses. One faction called for the school administration to close the street to motor vehicles in order to save lives, and when the school failed to take action, these protesters arrived late one night with mortar mix and concrete blocks, old tires, broken furniture, anything heavy they could pile into a barricade. By the next sunrise, 13th Avenue was blocked, and would stay blocked—first by the protesters, then by the concrete posts and planters I knew.

In the 1980s my student friends and I took part in the Primal Scream for Nuclear Disarmament—on designated dates, at designated moments late at night, we'd get loaded on beer and scream in unison for a full minute. At parties all over campus, all over Eugene, groups of students were pumping up pressure in beer kegs, tamping dope into bong bowls, chewing magic mushrooms, then throwing their heads back and howling into the backyard darkness at the exact same moment. A kind of weekly New Year's Eve, made noble by the idea that we were united in a political gesture for world peace.

When the film *The Gods Must Be Crazy* came to town, we torched the party bowls, drank the bong water, and marched the sidewalks outside the campus movie theater, picketing—white students protesting that the film should be banned as racist.

On any given day, when we could claim political expression and skip class, hundreds of us would lie down around the Student Union building, carpeting the ground in a "die-in" to protest nuclear proliferation. But only on weekdays, only in dry weather, and only in certain areas. Nobody wanted to pretend radioactive death in a mud puddle. No, we'd all die right after a big lunch, dead in the bright sunshine, our dead mouths smoking clove cigarettes, whispering clove-stinking gossip to each other or reading paperback copies of *The Monkey Wrench Gang*. When Democratic vice-presidential candidate Geraldine Ferraro came campaigning, we flopped down, dead, a smoking, tangled acre of stoned bodies spread around her.

Good times. The Berlin Wall. The Reagan years.

These were all staged rituals, little structured events we shared to create memories we could hold in common. These were small tests and challenges to help me and my peers develop our sense of power. Here was a safe, controlled way we could practice our effect on the larger world. Anyone who objected to our noble screaming at 3:00 AM, or who wanted to buy a ticket for *The Gods Must Be Crazy*, or who tried to wade through our dead bodies on their way to the cafeteria, well, those people were the enemy. We were united in our clove cigarettes and neon-colored punk clothing and little acts of shared transgression.

And a decade later, sitting with the publishers, those former hippy radicals who boasted about seizing power one night, blocking the flow of traffic and forever changing the map of a city, it seemed to me that the main benefit of their act had been how it allowed that group of people the permission and purpose to enjoy each other's company for a day's time. All those strangers, kids fresh off the farm or escaped from suburban homes, all these kids free of their families, they needed a reason to come together. They needed a simple structure. A mission or goal or game. They needed to know the roles they were to play. Otherwise, it would be too . . . iffy.

Maybe the events called "flash mobs" were the purest example of this need: a crowd; an arbitrary date, place, and task; a short-lived chance to meet others; and a shared memory to reinforce any future relationship.

We come from families, and eventually—with the birth of our children or the aging of our parents—we fall back into those same families. But in between, we have a chance to discover something different, maybe a new form of social structure. People ask me why I write about characters who seem to live on the margins of society, and my answer is always that the fringe is the future. Outside the mainstream, people are engaged in constant small experiments, testing new social models, new hierarchies, new personal identities. The most successful of those experiments—what begin as cults, fads, crazes, or manias—the ones that serve people best grow to become the next mainstream.

The fringe is the future.

No, my small-press friends never did publish that first manuscript, but they did publish a short story of mine. The afternoon I listened to them rehash the late 1960s and their barricade victory, I started writing a story about a new social experiment, a club where men could go to engage in consensual violence and begin to build their own self confidence while shedding their fear of . . . well, everything. The mission and rules of this new club seemed entirely arbitrary, just so long as the experiment allowed the members to come together for a short time. A regularly occurring community where the participants could abandon their normal lives and feel connected to their peers.

Church used to serve this function, of a place where people could go, a safe place where they could express their worst selves, then be forgiven and accepted back into their community for another week. Now most churches seem to have become places where people go to look their best, wear their nicest clothing. In the late 1950s, individuals suffering under racial segregation went to church for comfort; there they found each other and the power to take action. Perhaps that was the transition from finding community in religion to finding it in politics or therapy. Now, to vent and exhaust their worst fears, people go to addiction recovery groups, political protests, fight clubs.

No, the philosophy of *Fight Club* is beside the point. Sure, Tyler Durden says some things, but he must. He has to spout something to justify that time standing on top of his soapbox. What's important is that the people around him have a reason to gather, to discover that they all share the same fears, and to take gradual action. The group's effect on the world doesn't matter. What's important is how the group helps each individual build his sense of ability and confidence. As the individuals gain a sense of their own strength, wisdom, endurance, and courage—the organization dies. The organization is *supposed* to die.

My small-press friends have been married since college. They've run their own publishing house for decades. Every year they hold an outdoor camping party, an all-night party where hundreds sleep outside and watch meteor showers. Instead of hauling together concrete blocks, they plan for outdoor toilets, drinking water, air mattresses, live music, beer, food. It's not a protest, but it's the same high. A twenty-four-hour community. The experiment of their youth, now merged with their family. A hybrid.

Again, the philosophy is not the point. A political objective is not the point.

In Eugene, at the University of Oregon, students are now protesting the fact that 13th Avenue is closed. The protesters claim that ambulances and emergency vehicles must drive long distances around campus, and that this delay could cost human lives. The old concrete barriers, they claim, make the campus too insulated from the outside world. Too isolated. This new crop of students, strangers fresh from their farms and families, they say that if the school administration won't remove the barricades, then some night. . . .

Jesse Kavadlo is an associate professor of English and the Writing Center Director at Maryville University of St. Louis. He teaches courses in writing, American literature, and interdisciplinary topics such as rock and roll, superheroes, conspiracies, and monsters. He is the author of the book *Don DeLillo: Balance at the Edge of Belief* (Peter Lang, 2004) as well as a variety of essays on contemporary American fiction, cultural studies, and writing pedagogy. His work has appeared in academic anthologies and journals, including *Critique, Studies in 20th Century Literature, Studies in Popular Culture,* and *The Writing Lab Newsletter.* He earned his Ph.D. in English at Fordham University. In the movie version of his life, Jesse would cast himself with Edward Norton, not Brad Pitt.

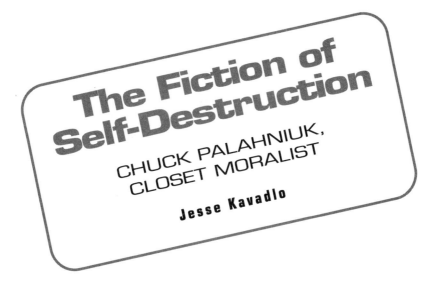

The Fiction of Self-Destruction
CHUCK PALAHNIUK, CLOSET MORALIST
Jesse Kavadlo

I magine what it's like to have your eyes rubbed raw with broken glass. This is what reading Chuck Palahniuk is like. You feel the shards in your eyes, yes, and then you're being punched, hard, your nose broken. Like the world is broken. Livid because there's violence, but also there's sex, there's the bodily fluid that accompanies violence and sex. Your eyes are rubbed in broken glass first, then in blood and lymph, and *you want more.* And that's just the plot! Don't even get me started on the characters. You should stop listening right now.

Okay, the characters are nameless dual-personality sadomasochistic anarchist neo-fascists turned rescuers. Or they're the last surviving members of a suicide cult turned domestic servants turned steroid-pumped Hollywood messiahs turned rescuers. Or they're sexually addicted self-loathing hypochondriac medical school dropout con artists (who pretend to choke in restaurants) turned rescuers. Not counting the one about the mangled former model and the transsexual who is really her brother but she doesn't know it, or the one about the mysterious crib deaths, or the one about the hidden rooms and human sacrifices. Don't count those. Count on fragments. And fragmentation. But somehow, you keep reading. And after you wipe the pulp from your eyes, you realize something. That the world is *not* broken. Somehow the world feels more together now than before you started. This is what it feels like to read Chuck Palahniuk. Broken, but something disturbing and beautiful recreated in its place. And when you're done, you realize that everything really is all right. When you're done, you find yourself thinking about the books. And, maybe, if you're lucky, sounding like them.

This essay will focus on the ways in which beauty, hope, and romance remain Palahniuk's central values throughout his seemingly ugly, existential, and nihilistic works, particularly in the novel and film *Fight Club*, Palahniuk's most widely recognized work, and *Survivor*, which I believe to be Palahniuk's strongest, most fully realized creation. That Palahniuk's harshest critics and most deferential fans mutually fail to notice these concerns becomes, I hope to show, central to the novels' aesthetic and moral imperatives.

— — —

Emerging at the end of the 1990s—the decade of the Republican Revolution, Susan Faludi's *Stiffed*, and the Angry White Male—Chuck Palahniuk rose to prominence in part because of the 1999 film adaptation of his novel *Fight Club* and in part because of his offbeat subject matter and animated prose style. With more than three hundred thousand copies of *Fight Club* in print, Palahniuk's following remains strong, particularly among young men, a demographic widely known to the publishing world for its reluctance to read. This appeal is unsurprising: Combining violent surrealism, suspenseful noir, and psychological and narrative twists, the novels depict middling men who find themselves raging against political, economic, and social systems.

Palahniuk's popularity is more complex, however, than chronological or cultural proximity to the Promise Keepers or Million Man March suggests. His books' manic charm transcends a core readership of disaffected young men galvanized by the books' stylish nihilism, violent chic, or tongue-in-cheek contravention. On the surface, the books celebrate testosterone-drenched, wanton destruction—*Fight Club*'s nameless narrator finds relief from stultifying consumerism by forming an underground boxing network, but the violence escalates to attempted bombings; *Survivor* revolves around twin conceits of cult suicides and narrator Tender Branson's reversely paginated countdown to a plane crash; *Choke* ends with the stones of the makeshift castle torn down and hurled at narrator Victor Mancini, who has deceived hundreds of well-intentioned would-be rescuers. (Notice both named narrators have male-tinged names, BranSON and MANcini.) On the other hand, despite this outward sadism, the pain inflicted on others, the violence in the novels also embodies a peculiarly masculine brand of masochism: "Maybe self-improvement isn't the answer," *Fight Club*'s narrator imagines. "Maybe self-destruction is the answer."

Yet the novels are less acts of fantasized revenge than elaborate rituals of self-ruin. In *Fight Club*, the narrator's injuries, we discover in the ending's twist, have all been self-inflicted, because he and his nemesis, Tyler Durden, are in fact the same person, two sides to a split personality. The narrator and Tyler turn their acts of sado-masochism into masochism alone. Palahniuk's narrators rebel against what the books position as the emasculating conformity of contemporary America (IKEA takes a bigger beating than the fight club's members), but what the narrator has really been fighting, literally and figuratively, is himself. Taken as a whole, Palahniuk's work rearranges Freudian sublimation, projection, and discontent with civilization; in *Fight Club*, rebellion against the social order is transposed cruelty against the self, not the reverse.

More than millennialism, masculinism, or even masochism, however, Chuck Palahniuk's fiction embodies what I would like to call "closet morality." As Palahniuk's fans know, until September 2003—well into his career—Palahniuk kept quiet about his homosexuality. At one point, fearing that her upcoming article would reveal that he was gay, Palahniuk angrily condemned *Entertainment Weekly* reporter Karen Valby on his fan Web site, The Cult. The article did not, it turned out, "out" him at all, and Palahniuk subsequently withdrew his comments from the Web site. In the ensuing years, Palahniuk's disclosure has not affected his perception or reception, nor, of course, should it. But the incident may provide a way of reading the novels: Now, unlike his sexuality, it is only Palahniuk's morality that remains an open secret. Apparently Palahniuk could more convincingly disclose his sexual orientation than his compassion, which, despite his own protestations, remains in the closet: "I'm not a nihilist. I'm a romantic. All of my books are basically romances; they're stories about reconnecting with community," a claim he has reiterated in several interviews.

Despite the novels' façades of fury, Palahniuk's sexuality seems obvious in retrospect; indeed, *New Yorker* film critic David Denby and Salon book critic Laura Miller (both disparagingly) noted *Fight Club's* homoeroticism, and Robert Alan Brook and Robert Westerfelhaus published "Hiding Homoeroticism in Plain View: The *Fight Club* DVD as Digital Closet" before Palahniuk came out. Of course, Palahniuk's sexuality is not important; instead, it is the concealment and subsequently dramatic means of revelation that provide an understanding of Palahniuk's particular—one might say *queer*—morality. In all of Palahniuk's novels, seemingly public, political acts of insurgence (not unlike outing oneself irately online, in spectacular, and spectacularly wrong, fashion) conceal that they are, in truth, long-suffering outlets for private, dispossessed spiritual desires (akin, for example, to concealed homosexuality). Palahniuk's closet morality manifests itself in the novels' subtexts and implications, rather than their context or language. Within his ostensible inclination to subvert literary and social mores—to offend the right with anti-consumerist, anti-family bromides, sex, and violence, and to alienate the left with potential misogyny and flirtation with fascism—Palahniuk places the romantic desire for connection, which even astute readers, in their enthusiasm or indignation, may miss. Amidst the novels' wreckage of bodies and buildings alike lie constructive, opposing forces to the inward and outward violence. Each novel at the time of this writing—*Fight Club*, *Invisible Monsters*, *Survivor*, and *Choke*, through *Lullaby*, *Diary*, and the recent *Haunted*, egregiously violent even by Palahniuk standards—ultimately proposes that what its characters, and all of us, need is . . . love. As Palahniuk writes in the introduction to his nonfiction collection *Stranger Than Fiction*, "In case you haven't already noticed, all my books are about a lonely person looking for some way to connect with other people." He clearly feels that people haven't noticed. And he's right.

On the surface, Palahniuk's novels seem to embody the textbook existentialist tendencies, as defined and codified by M.H. Abrams:

> . . . to view a human being as an isolated existent who is cast into an alien universe, to conceive the universe as possessing no inherent truth, value, or meaning, and to represent human life—in its fruitless search for purpose and meaning, as it moves from the nothingness whence it came toward the nothingness where it must end—as an experience which is both anguished and absurd.

More than an existential philosopher, however, Palahniuk is an American ironist in the tradition of Mark Twain, Nathanael West, Flannery O'Connor, Vladimir Nabokov, and Don DeLillo. Existence certainly seems futile and absurd when gratuitous brutality, infanticide, human sacrifice, suicide, and disfigurement come to seem banal and ordinary. Yet the characters' frequent celebrations and glorifications of masculinity, sex, individuality, and mayhem attempt to forge something palpable and real in a world where everything is a "copy of a copy of a copy" (*Fight Club*) or "the signifier outlasts the signified" (*Survivor*), a world of surreal simulacra. Through Palahniuk's dramatic irony, however, readers have the opportunity to feel the redemptive powers of feminism, love, cooperation, harmony, and storytelling, by inhabiting worlds where they are conspicuously, even absurdly, absent. Through his books' masculine embodiment but closeted feminist critique, their existentialist exterior that conceals the sentimentalism in the closet, Palahniuk conveys romantic notions in ways that aren't hackneyed, didactic, or unconvincing. (When *Fight Club*'s narrator finally reveals his attraction to Marla, she asks, "Not love?" His response: "This is a cheesy moment. . . . Don't push it.") Palahniuk uses the term "communication," but I would extend it into communion: peace and love, certainly, but also the need for spiritual embodiment, and even the possibility of salvation in a deadened world. To do so, Palahniuk substitutes black humor and muscular prose for excessive pathos and maudlin characterization. The problem becomes whether readers can get to the closeted moral and metaphorical significances beyond the books', readers', and even Palahniuk's own occasional macho posturing, again as evidenced against *Entertainment Weekly* reporter Valby.

— — —

In *Fight Club*, the narrator meets Tyler Durden, who seems to be everything that the narrator is not: aggressive, individualistic, charismatic, powerful. At the same time, however, Tyler's nihilistic Generation X critiques of an exhausted earth—"Recycling and speed limits are bullshit. . . . They're like someone who quits smoking on his deathbed"—and post-Nietzschean philosophies—"It's only after you've lost everything . . . that you're free to do anything"—have been taken too literally by both fans and critics alike. Durden is not a generational spokesperson; even within the fiction of *Fight Club* he is a fictional character, a hallucination, another kind of copy of a copy of a copy, his own simulacrum. While throughout much of the book the narrator is convinced by Tyler, and thus wants to "destroy everything beautiful I'd never have," by the end, through Marla Singer, his antagonist turned love interest, he can find solace only in his attempt to save, not destroy, the world. After almost two hundred pages of pummeling irony, he allows himself the sincerity to tell Marla, "I think I like you," and in the end, just as the building they occupy is poised to explode, Marla says, "It's not love or anything . . . but I think I like you, too." Fight club never saves the narrator, as he says it does early in the novel; instead, Marla does. But first the narrator, like the reader, has to look past Tyler Durden's allure to find her. When he can, the desire to destroy himself is rendered as another kind of fiction, replaced by his desire for Marla. Though wounded and institutionalized in the book's final pages, he—and Marla—survive. Tyler does not.

While critics and readers, like the narrator, naturally gravitate toward Tyler Durden, as the narrator reveals early on, "the gun, the anarchy, the explosion is really about Marla Singer." The narrator meets Marla—ironically, of course—in a support group for men with testicular cancer, which neither of them, obviously, has. Instead, the narrator has been attending support meetings for patients with terminal illnesses to fight his insomnia; Marla goes, as she says, "to have a real experience of death." The narrator's recollections of Marla, though, are consistently linked in the narrative to Big Bob (the film's opening cuts from one to the other), a former bodybuilder and the novel's only mother figure: Between his cancer and the resulting testosterone imbalance, Bob has huge breasts and no testicles. Like a mother, Bob uses his enormous breasts, hugs, and love to give the narrator his release, allowing him first to cry and then to sleep, which are both infantile needs. "Babies," the narrator tells us, "don't sleep this well." While Marla is busy as his pre-Durden adversary, the narrator receives maternal, feminine care from Bob's pendulous breasts.

Marla's presence at the meetings, though, eventually gives rise to the narrator's own lie, and soon he can no longer receive Bob's respite. As the narrator moves closer to his own, and society's, destruction, substituting the macho violence and bloodshed of fight club for the support group's castrated hugs and tears, Bob's breasts move from mothering to smothering: In the film, when the narrator meets Bob again in fight club, Bob's breasts become the source of his suffocation rather than his succor, and instead of falling blissfully to sleep, the narrator passes out. By now, both the narrator and Bob have a new love object: Tyler Durden.

Indeed, throughout most of the book, it is Tyler—and neither Bob the mother nor Marla the lover—who attracts and preoccupies the narrator. And what makes Durden attractive to the narrator—his potency, wit, and sly subversion—are the same qualities that appeal to a readership of solitary young men. Critics of the film find it ridiculous that buff Hollywood idol Brad Pitt, playing Durden, can sincerely recite lines like "We are the middle children of history, raised by television to believe that someday we'll be millionaires and movie stars and rock stars, but we won't." Henry Giroux calls it "a contradiction that cannot be overstated," and Salon's Andrew O'Hehir says "there's something more than a little ludicrous about sitting in a theater while Brad Pitt preaches at you about the emptiness of materialism."

What these critics see as contradictory or ludicrous, however, I see as comic irony to underscore the narrative drama. As attractive as Tyler seems (and that is the power of Pitt's casting), his philosophies are a fantasy and a delusion, as Tyler himself turns out to be. Even after discovering that he and Tyler are one, the narrator denies their connection in the novel: "I love everything about Tyler Durden, his courage and his smarts. His nerve. Tyler is funny and charming and forceful and independent, and men look up to him and expect him to change their world. Tyler is capable and free, and I'm not." Or as the film's Tyler/Pitt bluntly puts it: "All the ways you wish you could be, that's me. I look like you want to look, fuck like you want to fuck. I am smart, I am capable, and most importantly, I'm free in all the ways that you are not." An epitome of the American masculine ideal, Pitt is a perfect Tyler, exactly the star most men would wish to play them (to borrow a conceit from *Survivor*) in the movie version of their lives. As a result, however, we must never take Tyler literally; to do so would be madness, as it is for the narrator, or fascism, as it is for the members of Project Mayhem. Palahniuk's moral fiction conveys—but ultimately warns against—both.

Critics, however, take Tyler, like Pitt, at face value. In a scathing analysis, Giroux calls *Fight Club*

> [a] morally bankrupt and politically reactionary film.
> Representations of violence, masculinity, and gender

in *Fight Club* seem all too willing to mirror the pathology of individual and institutional violence that informs the American landscape, extending from all manner of hate crimes to the far right's celebration of paramilitary and protofascist subcultures.

Yet Giroux, I think, substitutes what the film and novel *depict* for what they ultimately *prescribe*. *Fight Club* rails against consumerist conformity, but its alternative, Project Mayhem, which evolves out of fight club—the "protofascist subculture," to use Giroux's term—takes far more of its members' individuality—names, clothes, hair, identities—than consumer culture can. That is, until Big Bob—one Robert Paulson—is inadvertently killed by a police officer during a prank gone wrong. The narrator, now aware that his followers believe him to be Tyler Durden, attempts to put an end to Project Mayhem, but realizes, echoing the language of fanatic religious martyrdom (in anticipation of *Survivor*) more than fascism, "only in death will we have our own names since only in death are we no longer part of the effort. In death we become heroes." The narrator, however, no longer believes this, and Palahniuk's irony thus subverts Giroux's reading—the book's endorsement of violence, rather than the narrator, self-destructs.

Giroux's reading is understandable. *Fight Club* dares its readers to take Tyler—and his reactionary politics—at face value. But in addition to rescuing Palahniuk from his detractors, he also needs rescuing from his admirers. More unsettling than Giroux's academic denunciation is the popular readership that identifies too strongly with Tyler Durden, exemplified by the angry, misogynistic letters Salon received after it published Laura Miller's scathing review of *Diary*. Yet again, fan reaction is understandable, if not excusable, considering Palahniuk's constant second-person "you" constructions—"You drill the wrong holes," "You don't understand any of it, and then you die," "That old saying, how you always kill the one you love, well, look, it works both ways"—which appear on the first three pages alone. This direct address, in its grammatical imperative, suggests the breakdown between the narrator and Tyler, and by extension, between character and reader, around which the novel revolves. Like the narrator, Tyler is alienated, angry, and politically, economically, and socially (although, crucially, not sexually) impotent. Judging by the online reviews and posts at sites like Amazon.com and The Cult, many fans emphasize how strongly they relate. Amazon.com reviews typically begin with a favorite Durden quote, yet some readers seem not to notice that he offers no viable or sustainable call for political creation, only metaphysical destruction—which, when enacted, becomes self-destruction.

In addition to these critical reactions and fan responses, there is Palahniuk's own penchant for bombast. In a personal response to Miller's negative review, Palahniuk wrote back: "Until you can create something that captivates people, I'd invite you to just shut up." Palahniuk's interviews sometimes resemble Durden's aphorisms, and his nonfiction has explored personal experiences with steroids, the occult, physical abuse, and the circumstances surrounding his father's extraordinary murder. And, of course, there was the *Entertainment Weekly* debacle.

It is thus tempting to read the narrators—and, by extension, the film *Fight Club*—as representative of Palahniuk's politics. The novels themselves, however, are not mouthpieces for their damaged narrators; they are critical of them. Palahniuk may be angry at the same violent social conditions that disturb *Fight Club*'s nameless narrator, *Survivor*'s Tender Branson, and *Choke*'s Victor Mancini, but Palahniuk's solution is not more violence—it is to write books. It's revealing that his letter to Miller also states that "it's easy to attack and destroy an act of creation. It's a lot more difficult to perform one," which emphasizes creation over destruction, as his books ultimately do as well. (The letter, however, like the Valby incident, was obviously self-destructive—as the letter even concedes, writers may be best off ignoring critics.) If Palahniuk's solution is books, his books' solution is laughter and romance. A careful reader will, like the narrator, be left unconvinced by Tyler's sophistry and instead notice that only his language, exemplified by Palahniuk's pumped-up, brutally funny style, is powerful. His solutions—to take the film's tagline: "Mischief. Mayhem. Soap"—are not.

Tyler Durden's indifference to suffering should not transfer onto the reader, who may identify with his position but also recoil, by the end, at his acts of violence. Even the narrator cannot remain morally neutral. If *Fight Club* embodies Giroux's protofascism, it is only in order to condemn it. In their brutality and futility, Tyler's followers, the nameless and faceless "space monkeys," blur the lines between rebellion and conformity with the zeal of conversion, discarding tie wearing, Starbucks sipping, and IKEA shopping to instead become mantra-repeating blackshirts. The book's crypto-fascism is not unambiguously 1960s-style anti-consumerism per se, Tyler's charisma (and Brad Pitt) notwithstanding. It is, rather, a call to recognize that fascism is the endgame of a capitalist system that would reduce workers to drones and all personal identification to brand names and commercial transactions. Even family is implicated in the depersonalized strictures: The narrator notes with his usual detachment that his father serially divorced and started a new family every six years: "This isn't so much like a family as it's like he sets up a franchise." The book's political subtext, far from right wing, insinuates that our cherished bastions of American liberty—the free market, liberal autonomy, and family values—come loaded with nascent totalitarianism.

The book establishes this potential for violence beneath each of its bland, bourgeois exteriors: because of the narrator's extortion, his morally bankrupt corporate workplace—which weighs the value of human lives against the cost of recalling a faulty automobile—finances the equivalently morally bankrupt Project Mayhem (this is more overt in the film than in the novel); everyday consumer products like gasoline, orange juice concentrate, or diet cola become reconfigured as napalm, among other chemical weapons or explosives; from the medical waste dump, "liposuctioned fat sucked out of the richest thighs in America" is rendered into expensive designer soap, to be sold "back to the very people who paid to have it sucked out." The potential for danger and destruction lurks beneath seemingly harmless merchandise and benign consumer culture. Similarly, Tyler Durden is the split personality that "just happen[s] to have the same fingerprints" as the narrator; he is the angry, murderous reverse of the innocuous pencil pusher. In the cultural logic of the closet, people and products alike have an unseen, balancing flipside that remains crucial to their identity, practice, and existence. Tyler's solution to corporate conformity and immorality, however, is anti-corporate conformity and immorality. The only viable alternative, then, is to reject modern masculinity's futile alienation and instead embrace connection, romanticism, and narrative, a seeming contradiction considering the novel's overtly male posturing, and its readership.

This is the Palahniuk paradox: The novels persuasively embody and give voice to the disenfranchised Angry White Male, only to critique him humorously, relentlessly, and morally from inside the novel's closet. Some readers may relate to or find truth in Tyler Durden's sarcasm and pop-hip existentialism—"you are not a beautiful and unique snowflake"—but like the unnamed narrator, the reader must ultimately banish him if he is to survive. He may be a part of us, but a part that must be healthily suppressed—or, as it were, closeted.

— — —

If *Fight Club* suggests a burgeoning tyranny lurking below the twin shimmering surfaces of consumerism and family, then *Survivor* extends the notion further. Here the distinctions between family and faction, and between consumerism and cult, are eroded entirely. Tender Branson appears to be the last surviving member of the Creedish, or, as the media rename it, the Creedish Death Cult, for its members have all committed suicide. As the book opens, Tender is recording his life story into the black box of a plane he has hijacked, to be crashed into the Australian outback. Between the countdown and the expected crash, the book leaves few taboos untouched: suicide, murder, prostitution, pornography, religion, and television all receive the same irreverent, satirical treatment.

Like Durden, Tender Branson (a near cryptogram of "Tyler Durden," by the way) frequently seems to channel Nietzsche, yet again I don't feel as though we should take his philosophy—"there is no heaven. There is no Hell. . . . Now anything is possible," or later, "this is the upside of being eternally damned"—literally. Here, we understand the remarks to be the opposite of Nietzsche's poorly understood "God is dead" pronouncement: The narrator is more controlled, less powerful, than ever. Even in the absence of his once-believed religious absolutes, Tender believes more strongly in a universal order, a scheme of unchanging grand narratives, than he ever did as a cult member. He is the opposite of Nietzsche's *übermench*: weak-willed, weak-minded, controlled mentally, emotionally, physically. As the TV guru he is manipulated into becoming, he can parrot the jargon of self-empowerment as easily as *Fight Club*'s narrator could as a support group faker, but Tender is also a "tourist," always reading someone else's words in his teleprompter. Neither the cult of family nor the cult of American celebrity offers him relief from his fear of death and fear of life, but his love interest, Fertility Hollis, does—not because she's omniscient, but because, in the end, she is not.

Unlike *Fight Club*'s unnamed narrator, Tender Branson's name is suffused with significance. As the novel explains, Tender is "not really a name. It's more of a rank. . . . It's the lowest rank. . . . Tenders are workers who tend." In the rigid hierarchy of the Creedish, the role of each son after the first (who is always named Adam) is to tend to others' needs. In addition, though, according to the *Oxford Pocket Dictionary*, "tender," as an adjective, means "easily cut or chewed, not tough; susceptible to pain or grief; sensitive, delicate, fragile; loving and affectionate." As Tender actively encourages desperate people to kill themselves ("try barbiturates and alcohol with your head inside a dry-cleaning bag"), he does not immediately seem to qualify as "tender." But the word also means "requiring tact or careful handing," and Tender is indeed carefully handled throughout the novel, first by his church elders, then by his depraved employers, then by his manager, and finally by Fertility Hollis. And despite his outward hardness and meanness, Tender is indeed tender—loving and affectionate, as well as susceptible to pain and grief. Like Palahniuk's closeted sexuality, *Survivor*'s tenderness—ostensibly absurd in a character who is a victim and victimizer, who is manipulated and who manipulates so many—is in the closet yet in plain sight: in its narrator's name.

Despite any tenderness, though, Palahniuk's moral imperative directs his social criticism toward greater targets than fringe religions. As the book progresses, it becomes clear that whatever obvious criticism Palahniuk proffers toward the Creedish, those same criticisms apply to mainstream American culture. When Tender Branson remembers the thousands of cooking and cleaning instructions that he learned in order to be of service to his future employers, he understands that the teaching "made us stupid. . . . With all the little facts we learned, we never had time to think. None of us ever considered what life would be like cleaning up after a stranger day after day. Washing dishes all day. Feeding a stranger's children. Mowing a lawn. Painting houses. Year after year. Ironing bedsheets." Add the possibility of also going to a *Fight Club*–style corporate job, substitute "husband," "wife," or "children" for "stranger," and the complaint is typically middle-class American. Finally, "tender" is also a verb, meaning "to offer or present," with its accompanying nouns, "bid, proposal," as in legal tender (this very phrase is used in the novel itself). And that, in Palahniuk's social and moral criticism, is what Tender Branson, like too many Americans, has let himself become: a kind of legal tender, a means to an end, living capital ready for exchange, whether cleaning a house, urging suicide, or, later, telling people the proper spiritual way to live. Tender, like too many Americans, is indistinguishable from his tasks.

Tender begins to understand that everything he had been taught was fabricated, as artificial as the fake flowers that inspire him and that he tends with the zeal usually associated with the care of the living. Of course, since they are not alive, "the best place to find bulbs for forcing is in the Dumpster behind the mausoleum." While there, Tender wishes to be "chased by flesh-eating zombies," out of the romantic, wistful yearning that "it would prove some sort of life after death." The notion is tender—immature (another meaning of "tender")—but suggestive of his emotional fragility and susceptibility to existential pain. The book then becomes a black-comic update of Keats's "Ode on a Grecian Urn": Palahniuk examines the ironic tension between the immortal perfection and perfectibility of art—or, for Palahniuk, the fake, the artificial, the simulation—versus life's flaws and finiteness. As the novel continues, Tender becomes a false prophet but makes real profits, in the process buffing his body with a StairMaster (a kind of artificial exercise) and chemical supplements, wearing a wig when the supplements make his hair fall out, capping his teeth, bronzing his skin, reading the words off a teleprompter, learning about cures that exist in name only (but "of course they're real"), and attending his own televised, fake wedding (no love, no ring, no spoken words, and even the ostensibly fake bride is replaced at the last minute by an understudy), so that, as Tender says of the flowers, "from a distance, everything looks perfect." "Perfect," while fine for fakes, by the end demoralizes Tender.

Palahniuk's signature plot twists extend the trope of artificiality further: Tender's long-lost brother Adam is revealed as a murderer; Tender is a wanted man; and Adam, Tender, and Fertility Hollis invent a fictional terminally ill child and live in prefabricated houses before winding up in the Tender Branson Sensitive Materials Sanitary Landfill (a pornography junk yard), where Tender kills Adam at his request. Finally, Fertility pulls from her bag real flowers: "These flowers will be rotten in a couple hours. Birds will crap on them. The smoke here will make them stink, and tomorrow a bulldozer will probably run them over, but for now they are so beautiful." The life of the real flowers, however temporary and imperfect, is preferable to the artificial ones that haunt Tender, the mausoleum, and the novel's pages.

While *Survivor* begins with seeming trivia about how to "get bloodstains out of a fur coat" ("the secret is cornmeal and brushing the fur the wrong way"), "get blood off piano keys," "hide bullet holes in a living-room wall," "repair stab holes in nightgowns, tuxedoes, and hats," or use "green-tinted moisturizer [to] help hide red, slapped skin," these bits become another, if opposite, version of *Fight Club*'s homemade recipes for napalm and explosives: In *Fight Club*, behind the faces of regular, everyday products lie the means for terror and violence, much like the men who inhabit the world of *Fight Club* itself. Here, behind the world of stain removal or hole repair is the inescapable fact of bloodshed, a bullet fired, a knife used, skin slapped. *Fight Club* uses seemingly harmless merchandise to expose the potential for violence; *Survivor* uses everyday products to conceal the violence that has already been inflicted. Somehow, soap and cleanliness are never next to godliness, and "the copy of a copy of a copy," at least suggestive of an original, gives way to sanitized suppression in the name of perfection. Tender's cleaning tips in the novel's opening lead directly to the conclusion's porn landfill, the *reductio ad absurdum* of American hypocrisy, secrecy, obsessive compulsion, and misophobia.

Yet Tender continues to survive his mistreatment at the hands of his family, the cult, his employers, his caseworker, and his manager. He continues to tell the tale, even as the reader, more than in a conventional novel, is constantly reminded of the story's ending and finiteness by Palahniuk's reverse pagination (the story opens on 289 and ends on page 1). The countdown appears to be to the plane crash, explosion, and death, even as the novel concludes contentedly: "The sun is total and burning and just right here, and today is a beautiful day." That sentiment is far more Zen than existential, and, like Fertility's live flowers, suggests the immediate, divine, and sublime element of the present moment. To conclude, Tender both celebrates and laments the power of narrative: "It's all done. It's all just a story now," finishing in circular fashion, with the same "Testing, testing, one, two—" of the opening, a dash substituting for the completion that "three" provided on the first page. The reader has no way to know whether Tender has miraculously survived, or whether the last dash is the final crash.

Ever the closet moralist, however, Palahniuk revealed his "real" ending on The Cult's Web site:

> The end of *Survivor* isn't nearly so complicated. It's noted on page 7(8?) [sic] that a pile of valuable offerings has been left in the front of the passenger cabin. This pile includes a cassette recorder. Even before our hero starts to dictate his story—during the few minutes he's supposed to be taking a piss—he's actually in the bathroom dictating the last chapter into the cassette recorder. It's just ranting, nothing important

> plot-wise, and it can be interrupted at any point by the destruction of the plane. The minute the fourth engine flames out, he starts the cassette talking, then bails out, into Fertility's waiting arms (she's omniscient, you know). The rest of the book is just one machine whining and bitching to another machine. The crash will destroy the smaller recorder, but the surviving black box will make it appear that Tender is dead. ("The Ending of *Survivor*")

It is curious that Palahniuk did not include this section in the novel itself. The reader, without this information, could fairly assume that Tender dies, although the book presents no way to show his death, since he himself is narrating. (The ending's dash, however, reminiscent of Emily Dickinson's many poems about death, doesn't bode well.) The reverse pagination suggests a countdown to the crash, as opposed to the takeoff. But this optimistic ending is revealed in almost exactly the same manner as Palahniuk's sexuality: available on his Web site, but specifically and deliberately hidden to all but Palahniuk's fifteen thousand closest online confidants.

— — —

Unlike their narrators, who always experience a change of heart, Palahniuk's novels ultimately enact their own self-destruction, through their self-deconstruction—the ironic sense that the reader's cultural views by the end of the novel should be precisely the opposite of the views expressed by the narrator at the beginning, a kind of moral chiasmus. Again and again, the supposedly espoused machismo, masochism, and nihilism must be traded hastily for something else, and that "something else" seems consistently to be love. Once Palahniuk's narrators learn the truths about themselves, they turn to their love interests for redemption. In *Fight Club*, we must go back to the beginning and relearn the novel from the new perspective that the narrator and Tyler Durden are one, or in *Survivor* that the barren Fertility Hollis is pregnant with Branson's baby, or that *Choke's* "Dr." Paige Marshall, the novel's medical and moral guide, is really a patient in an insane asylum, and so on. The stories, like the characters, self-destruct—but never completely. There's just enough left of them, and the narrative, to begin rebuilding, which is the very image that concludes *Choke*.

Palahniuk has pioneered a new genre, the fiction of self-destruction. The subject and subtext for all his novels is, of course, self-destruction—fight clubs, explosions, and deliberate plane crashes suggest little else—but the novels themselves philosophically and narratively self-destruct as well, in their recurring irony and twist endings. Even the trope of self-destruction self-destructs—the stories that we thought we had read always turn out to be another kind of fiction—and despite bullet wounds to the head (*Fight Club* and *Invisible Monsters*), car crashes and bombs (*Fight Club*), angry mobs (nearly all books), a potential plane crash (*Survivor*), and bowel obstruction and public stoning (*Choke*), Palahniuk's characters are really hardy survivors, and the books, for all their shock and controversy, have fewer deaths than the average airport-bookstore thriller (*Haunted* and *Lullaby* are the exceptions). And when characters do die, such as *Fight Club*'s Bob or even Branson's goldfish, it retains its power to upset.

In the end, the books render the concept of self-destruction as unreliable and unsustainable as the bombs that fail to detonate at the end of *Fight Club*. In the film, of course, the bombs do explode, and the buildings indeed crumble, in pre-9/11 imagery that would surely never have been produced just a few years later. At the same time, however, the film ironically uses the metaphor to fortify, rather than demolish, the final romance between Marla and the narrator, by using the bursting bombs and imploding buildings as the literal backdrop to their replete romance, their explosive embrace. Their world, rather than ending, is just beginning. The film concludes with the humorous shot of the "subliminally" spliced-in image of the penis, reminding viewers of the film's much-touted masculinity, but more importantly of the main characters' emerging sexuality and, self-reflexively, that what we're seeing is really just a movie. The romantic-rock soundtrack plays, the credits roll, and astute viewers experience the shock of recognition that *Fight Club* turned out to be, of all things, an uplifting movie.

If Palahniuk is ultimately too romantic to be an existentialist, perhaps that means that critics, including Abrams, have been too quick to characterize existentialism through the lens of Camus's *Myth of Sisyphus*: "In a universe that is suddenly deprived of illusion and light, man feels a stranger. His is an irremediable exile. . . . This divorce between man and his life, the actor and his setting, truly constitutes the feeling of Absurdity." Jean-Paul Sartre comes closer to characterizing Palahniuk's moral fiction in his essay "What Is Literature?":

> However bad and hopeless the humanity which it paints may be, the work must have an air of generosity. Not, of course, that this generosity is to be expressed by means of edifying discourses and virtuous characters; it must not be premeditated, and it is quite true that fine sentiments do not make fine books. But the very warp and woof of the book, the stuff out of which people and things are cut; whatever the subject a sort of essential lightness must appear everywhere and remind us that the world is never a natural datum, but an *exigence* and a *gift*. . . . Thus, the writer's universe will only reveal itself in all its depth to the examination, the admiration, and the indignation of the reader; and the generous love is a promise to maintain and the generous indignation is a promise to change . . . ; although literature is one thing and morality quite a different one, at the heart of the aesthetic imperative we discern the moral imperative.

And indeed, despite his efforts to closet them, we do understand that with Palahniuk's aesthetic imperative—and his style and language are truly original—comes a moral imperative, as well: that we must communicate, love one another, and survive. Unlike Camus,

Chuck Palahniuk is generous, and no one's exile seems irremediable. If anything, the opposite is true: The novel's circular construction always returns the plot, and its narrator, to the original point of exile. In the closet of postmodern apocalypses and existential absurdities, Palahniuk's novels are old-fashioned romances. But they're not decked out in Brad Pitt–as–Tyler Durden's neo-hipster get-up. Tyler's vintage denim, red leather, wraparound shades, and mussed pomade hairdo exist only in the film; when the narrator meets him in the book, Tyler is naked. Palahniuk may nod to designer nihilism, but he knows that the emperor has no clothes. Ever moral, Palahniuk instead insists that despite their appetites for self-destruction, his characters—and, by extension, his readers—must live.

Works Cited

Abrams, M.H. *A Glossary of Literary Terms* seventh ed. Fort Worth: Harcourt, 1999.

Brook, Robert Alan and Robert Westerfelhaus. "Hiding Homoeroticism in Plain View: The *Fight Club* DVD as Digital Closet": *Critical Studies in Media Communication* 19, no. 1, March 2002, 21–43.

Chalmers, Robert. "Chuck Palahniuk: Stranger than Fiction." *Independent*, online edition. August 1, 2004. <http://enjoyment.independent.co.uk/books/interviews/article49383.ece>

The Cult Web site. <http://205.196.209.178>

Giroux, Henry A. *Public Spaces, Private Lives: Beyond the Culture of Cynicism*. Lanham, Maryland: Rowman and Littlefield, 2001.

O'Hehir, Andrew. "Fight Club." Salon. October 15, 1999. <http://dir.salon.com/ent/movies/review/1999/10/15/fight_club/index.html?sid=350202>

Palahniuk, Chuck. "The Ending of *Survivor*." The Cult. <http://205.196.209.178/books/survivor/survivorending.php>

———. Interview by Laura J. Williams. *The Fresh Take* 2, no. 2. September 2004. <http://www.annarborpaper.com/ content/issue24/palahniuk_24.html>

————. Letter to the Editor. Salon.com. August 26, 2003. (Accessed February 11, 2005.) <http://archive.salon.com/books/letters/2003/08/26/chuck>

————. *Stranger Than Fiction: True Stories*. New York: Doubleday, 2004.

————. *Survivor*. New York: Anchor, 1999.

Sartre, Jean Paul. "What Is Literature?" *Norton Anthology of Theory and Criticism*, Vincent B. Leitch. ed. New York: Norton, 2001. 1336–1349.

Christopher N. Chandler is a Ph.D. candidate in Divinity at St. Andrews University. His current research concerns corruption and poverty issues in the life of Jesus and the New Testament, and his future work involves development in Sierra Leone—the poorest country in the world.

Philip Tallon is a Ph.D. candidate in Divinity at St. Andrews University. His essay on *Psycho* recently appeared in *Hitchcock and Philosophy*, from Open Court Press.

Poverty and Anarchy in Fight Club

Christopher N. Chandler and Philip Tallon

David Fincher's provocative 1999 film *Fight Club* goes toe to toe, bare knuckled, with a number of philosophical issues. Nietzschean volitionalism, personal identity, the eventual disintegration of reality—these are pressing issues for anyone who takes the film seriously.

But Fincher's film also raises crucial questions about the issue of debt in our culture and how to handle it. Therefore, we seek answers to the question: "What is Tyler Durden's philosophy of debt and material wealth?" Is Tyler just an anarchist with a penchant for making soap, or could he be on to something? To tackle this question, we begin with a sketch of the main character's dual personality.

IKEA Boy's Identity Crisis

The nineties neologism "wageslave" fits the main character (the nameless "Jack") like a tailored suit. Seated on the toilet, holding a magazine vertically, he explains, "Like so many others I had become a slave to the IKEA nesting instinct." As Jack describes each individual item of his lust—"the Erika Pekkari dust ruffles, the Klipsk personal office unit, the Hovetrekke home exerbike"—his apartment fills. "I'd flip through a catalogue and wonder, 'What kind of dining set defines me as a person?' We used to read pornography. Now it was the Horchow collection." Ordering so many "versatile solutions for modern living" undoubtedly pushes him into the black hole of credit card debt. Yet his pursuit of material fulfillment is unshakable. The loss of Jack's suitcase while on a business trip distresses him: "I had everything in that suitcase. My CK shirts. My DKNY shoes. My A/X ties." When the arson unit calls, Jack laments the loss of his material possessions: "That condo was my life, Ok," Jack says to the detective. "I loved every stick of furniture in that place. That was not just a bunch of stuff that got destroyed. It was me!"

Jack, the corporate slave, defines himself by his material possessions, and by what he does from nine to five to attain those things. Enter Jack's alter ego Tyler Durden. Jack's question to Tyler is telling: "What do you *do?*" But Tyler questions Jack's question: "What do you mean?" Tyler's self-identity is so purely noncorporate that Jack must explain, "What do you do *for a living?*" Tyler does not work for a corporation. "I make and I sell soap. The yardstick of civilization."

The contrast between these two identities becomes even clearer when the two talk in a bar, after Jack's apartment has just exploded. "I don't know," Jack says, quivering, "it's just when you buy furniture you tell yourself that's it. That's the last sofa I'm gonna need. Whatever else happens, I've got that sofa problem handled. I had it all. I had a stereo that was very decent. A wardrobe that was getting very respectable. I was so close to being complete."

The conversation turns as Tyler begins to press Jack on his catalogue lifestyle.

"Do you know what a duvet is?" asks Tyler. "It's a blanket. Just a blanket. Now why do guys like you and I know what a duvet is? Is this essential to our survival . . . in the hunter-gatherer sense of the word? No. What are we then?"

Like a schoolboy guessing at his first geometry problem, Jack mumbles, "Consumers?"

"Right. We are consumers. We are byproducts of a lifestyle obsession. Crime, murder, poverty—these things don't concern me. What concerns me are celebrity magazines, television with five hundred channels, some guy's name on my underwear. Rogaine, Viagra, Olestra."

"Martha Stewart," Jack mumbles, trying to think like a free man.

"Fuck Martha Stewart. Martha's polishing the brass on the *Titanic*. It's all going down, man. So fuck off with your sofa unit and Strinne green stripe patterns. I say never be complete. I say stop being perfect. I say let's evolve. Let the chips fall where they may."

"It's just stuff," Jack says, aligning his priorities in life an inch closer to Tyler's.

"Well, you did lose a lot of versatile solutions for modern living," Tyler says with light irony.

"My insurance is probably gonna cover it, so . . ." Jack reverts while Tyler stares at him in disbelief. Realizing Tyler's disapproval, he asks, "What?"

"The things you own end up owning you."

— — —

These two personalities are polar opposites. Since Tyler is "free in all the ways that Jack is not," he begins liberating Jack from his slavery to consumption by opening Jack's eyes to the world of "rock bottom"—living, that is, not prices. Since his luxury apartment with "floor-to-ceiling windows" blows up, sending his personal effects sailing "flaming into the night," Jack gives up the posh condo life to live with Tyler in "a dilapidated house in a toxic waste part of town." Drawing on primal anger and economic angst, they start a movement to liberate others from corporate slavery.

This struggle between "corporate Jack" and "noncorporate Tyler" continues right to the ending scene. Jack pleads with Tyler to call off the impending demolition of the credit card buildings. Insulting Jack with the derogatory epithet "IKEA Boy," Tyler remains unrepentant. "What do you want? You want to go back to your shit job? Fucking condo world watching sitcoms? Fuck you! I won't do it." Tyler that opposes the corporate world Jack is enslaved by.

Debt and Poverty on Planet Starbucks

While Jack and Tyler represent diametrically opposed financial worldviews, a similar dualism is created in the movie between the poor working class and rich corporations. Outside of the corporate world, characters like Bob and Marla are depicted as poverty-stricken. Not only had Bob's venture into a late-night get-rich-quick scheme left him without any manhood, it also left him bankrupt. When Jack asks Marla why she deceptively attends a variety of support groups, she replies, "It's cheaper than a movie and there's free coffee." Her wardrobe is defined by what hangs on the thrift store racks. She survives by stealing clothes out of Laundromats and selling them at pawn shops, or by swiping meals from trucks delivering food to elderly shut-ins. "Tragically, they're dead," Marla coldly explains. "I'm alive and I'm in poverty." When Marla fears she has breast cancer and Jack advises her to go to a hospital, her response is, "I can't afford to throw money away on a doctor." Moreover, Tyler's movement is made up mostly of blue-collar workers. The clash between upper-class capitalism and lower-class struggle is set up by this contrast.

The corporation's role is one of creating and/or perpetuating poverty by being at the top of the hierarchy, controlling the profits. "When deep space exploration ramps up it'll be the corporations that name everything . . . the IBM Stellar Sphere, the Microsoft Galaxy, Planet Starbucks." Tyler sells his soap to department stores at twenty dollars a bar. But "God knows what *they* charged" is Jack's commentary. The airline industry collides midair with the insurance business in Jack's cynical, matter-of-fact admixture of the two. "Life insurance pays off triple if you die on a business trip," he says, and the message is clear: Corporate profits are valued more highly than human lives. The worker bees definitely need a haiku poem.

By day, Jack works for an insurance company that cares more about bottom-line profits than the number of lives lost each year due to its policies. The unethical cause of these deaths is described with a sterile math equation: "Take the number of vehicles in the field, A. Multiply it by the probable rate of failure, B. Then multiply the result by the average out-of-court settlement, C. A times B times C equals X. If X is less than the cost of a recall . . . we don't do one." This lack of concern for human welfare in favor of material possessions is satirically typified in Jack's boss, who knowingly commits these atrocities while selfishly satisfying his aesthetic desire for all things "cornflower blue."

The rhetoric of day-to-day business life is used to candy-coat corporate atrocities. When Jack's boss tells him to make the "red flags" his "primary action items," what he really means is something like, "You need to cover up this mess we're making in society and prevent any potential lawsuits." Corporate employees are made to follow senseless policies as a way to avoid litigation and prevent someone who has been wronged by a corporation from getting some of said corporation's profits. "Of course it's company policy never to imply ownership," Jack is informed. "In the event of a dildo we have to use the indefinite article *a* dildo, never . . . *your* dildo." Jack listens to a consultant spew worn-out corporate lines like, "Efficiency is priority number one people . . . because waste is a thief." The irony in this last line betrays a corporate world voraciously squeezing everything out of every possible person and resource available.

In the world of *Fight Club*, it is the corporation that is the wasteful thief, producing and promoting useless expensive items such as the bridesmaid's dress, which "someone loved . . . intensely for one day . . . then tossed." There is no real concern for those at the bottom of this pyramid. Jack's glass dishes are "crafted by the honest, simple, hard-working, indigenous peoples of . . . wherever." When Marla calls Jack after not seeing him at their support groups for a while, she informs him, "I've been going to debtors anonymous. You wanna see some really fucked up people. . . ." The world of capitalism, expressed through the corporation, devastates those at the bottom.

This greedy corporate world also attempts to define everyone. Tyler waxes eloquent: "Advertising has us chasing cars and clothes . . . working jobs we hate so we can buy shit we don't need." "I felt sorry for guys packed into gyms trying to look like how Calvin Klein or Tommy Hilfiger said they should," Jack later tells us.

You Are Not Your Fucking Khakis: Tyler's Liberating Worldview

Therefore, because this slavery to the cycle of work and consumption has resulted in Jack's "sick desperation," he slowly moves away from the corporate life. He stops wearing a tie to work. He smokes in the office and walks around the halls with "bruises from fighting." Eventually he starts a brawl with the corporate world itself. To fulfill his assignment from Tyler, Jack picks a fight with his boss. "Under and behind and inside everything this man took for granted"—the camera pans to the man's business card, then to his phone off the hook, then to the name plate on his desk—"something horrible had been growing." The security of the material and corporate culture with which Jack's boss had insulated himself is violently torn down—it is merely "the illusion of safety." Losing a fight to his boss is a major step away from corporate life for Jack.

While a computer store explodes in slow motion, Tyler preaches: "You are not your job. You are not how much money you have in the bank. You're not the car you drive. You're not the contents of your wallet. You're not your fucking khakis." The ideology that one's genuine identity can be discovered through status and the accumulation of material possessions within the larger matrix of the corporate world is obliterated like the computer monitors behind him.

In *Fight Club*—as in the larger fictional world of most books by Chuck Palahniuk—work is often seen as the most degrading of necessities. Throughout Palahniuk's canon we find people whose sole view of work is to earn money, and hence derive no sense of personal satisfaction from a "job well done." Inside and outside of *Fight Club*, no differentiation is made by Palahniuk between honest and dishonest work—*all* work is dishonest. In *Lullaby* we find a calculating realtor who sells and resells the same haunted houses, making quick money through systematic deception, and a scam artist who makes money by threatening successful businesses with bad press. In *Choke*, the protagonist, besides working a degrading job at a historically themed amusement park, pretends to choke on food night after night in order to bilk money out of sympathetic people. *Fight Club*'s view of vocation fits with this overall idea perfectly. If Jack's corporate job is immoral and degrading, then blackmailing the company is an improvement: at least it's not degrading.

Therefore, in place of the oppressive corporate system, an alternative community is built. This community is the opposite of the corporate world, which is enslaving, lonely, hierarchical, discriminatory, and uncompassionate. This alternative brotherhood is characterized by freedom, solidarity, decentralization, egalitarianism (both financially and racially), and respect for human life. Though there are elements of consumerist language present in Project Mayhem (the fight clubs that Tyler sets up all over the country are referred to as "franchises," and the pinnacle of the activities of these groups is likened to "pay-per-view"), people in this new life are not enslaved by the debts of the modern world. There are no car or house mortgages. And that's because this new community has a new philosophy. While Jack is on the phone with Detective Stern from the arson unit, Tyler shouts it like a drill sergeant: "Tell him the liberator who destroyed my property has realigned my perceptions! We reject the basic assumptions of civilization, especially those of material possessions!"

In keeping with this principle, it takes no money to become a member of a fight club. When Tyler talks with Lou, the greedy businessman who owns the tavern where fight club is held every night, Lou asks:

> "How much money [is Irvine] getting for this?"
> "There is no money," Tyler replies.
> "Free?" Lou exclaims.
> "Free to all," Tyler affirms.
> "Ain't that something!"

Tyler's retort—"It is, actually"—defines the spirit of this alternative philosophy of life.

In contrast to the "single-serving friends" of Jack's world, Tyler's house becomes a living organism teeming with brothers ready to give up food, water, money, and encouragement—ready even to die—for the same cause. Their goal is to correct the imbalances of power, position, and money created by the corporate world. The issue of finding a solution to being enslaved by debt has been addressed variously by philosophers, thinkers, and religions the world over. But to what specifically are we to compare *Fight Club's* philosophy of material possessions?

Tylers of the Past: Revolutions Against Debt in History

Economic inequity is as old as recorded history itself. In the ancient world, loans were given at rates of interest anywhere from 10 to 120 percent, depending on the type of loan (grain, precious metals), time of year, and economic conditions. More often than not, the rates were unmanageably high. In agrarian economies, it was quite easy for a farmer who had a bad crop to default on a seed loan and lose his land and freedom to a wealthy creditor. He became a literal slave. Slavery of this kind was a large socioeconomic class in antiquity, and the slave was physically branded with a mark of ownership. (Tyler might find it subversively ironic that we use the term "brands" to describe the outward symbols that "enslave" us today.) It is into this ancient milieu that two early reformers came: Solon in Athens and Nehemiah in Jerusalem.*

Both of these civic and religious leaders saw economic crises in which large masses of people were faced with losing everything— early versions of an impending stock market crash. In response, both Solon and Nehemiah canceled current debts, abolished slavery for debts, and brought back debtors who had been carried off as

---

*For a good overview of these two figures in their ancient context, see Edwin M. Yamauchi, "Two Reformers Compared: Solon of Athens and Nehemiah of Jerusalem" in *Bible World.*

slaves by foreign creditors. Solon even augmented the Athenian monetary system so as to create more financial equality. These leaders opposed the unjust amassing of wealth at the expense of the less-well-to-do masses.

Another early example of debt release is the institution of Jubilee laws in Hebrew society. These laws prescribed the release of land lost to creditors every fifty years and the forgiveness of financial debts every seven years. The Jubilee laws—if they arose from the grassroots of Hebrew society rather than from top-down legislation—can perhaps be compared to the English Common Law tradition we have today. In an agrarian world largely built on slave labor, one can see how attractive such laws (and thus religion) might have been.* Into situations of poverty and reform, however, comes a less peaceful means of social balancing.

When debt is perpetuated by giving the poor a false sense of hope and a "way out" through loans, these unfulfilled expectations of liberty combine with increasing debts and pile into a hopeless mass, resulting in an increasing sense of desperation. If an opportunity presents itself in the form of a weak central power or local law, the solution to the eradication of the debt is sometimes public, violent revolution.

Anarchy and revolt are some of the more radical ways those who feel trapped in a financial system have sought to redress this social discord. One ancient episode is the Jewish revolt of 66 CE. The Jewish people in first-century Palestine were heavily taxed by both the Roman government and their own local religio-civic leaders. The "office building" of these local elites—the Temple in Jerusalem—was a first-century version of the modern high-rise. This edifice, which was destroyed in 70 CE, was made of massive stones covered in gold. Marble pillars adorned its porticoes. The irony, however, is that many who paid to support such a structure languished in poverty. During one of Rome's civil wars, the poorer priests and the desperate peasants in Jerusalem saw an opportunity to get out from under

---

*On Jubilee, see Lev 25 and Deut 15. There is scholarly debate over the degree to which Jubilee was institutionalized and/or practiced in Hebrew society.

their crushing debt. They stormed the palaces of both the local king and the high priest, and then turned to the Temple where the financial archives and debt notes were kept. They quickly "burned the contracts belonging to their creditors" so as to "dissolve their obligations for paying their debts." The ancient Jewish historian Josephus explains that an insurrection followed: "This was done in order to gain the multitude of those who had been debtors and that they might persuade the poorer sort to join in their insurrection with safety against the more wealthy; so the keepers of the records fled away, and the rest set fire to them" (Josephus, *War of the Jews*). This is but one example from ancient history. Violent revolts have certainly also grown out of more modern times and philosophies.

Hegel, whose positivistic philosophy states that things are constantly evolving (dialectically) into better and better states, saw private property—in contrast to Tyler Durden's view—as a means of enabling this dialectical progression of freedom through various stages: from particular desires (being "in itself") to rational reflection (being "for itself") to rational actualization of one's desires (being "for others"). Hegel, ever the optimist, also saw the state as the source of our understanding of what is right (*Philosophy of Right*).

Hegel also inspired a number of followers who were less optimistic about the status quo. The most famous of the neo-Hegelians is, undoubtedly, Marx—a trenchant physical monist. Marx saw a great disharmony between an individual's labor and the capitalist system in which the laborer works. The control the capitalist has over the laborer is the core of the problem for Marx. He theorized that capitalism is a self-destructive economic system because the poor proletariat will inevitably rise up and displace those currently in positions of power and oppression. Marx also believed that religion—the "opiate of the people"—is used to legitimize this oppression and dupe people into social passivity.

Tyler's philosophy is certainly not one of evolution leading to a supreme or perfect state of affairs, as Hegelian thought suggests. His is a kind of "devolution" of both man and society, in which technology and progress are shunned so humans are enabled to return to an Eden-like state. Perhaps here Tyler's view can be seen as a kind of anti-Hegelian dialectic—a moving backward from artificial harmony between the self and others to a disharmony and competition at the most basic level.* Where Hegel sees property as enabling human perfection, Tyler seems to indicate the opposite. Not only is *debt* a burden to humans under Tyler's view, *property* is as well. Tyler's impassioned plea—"I say stop being perfect. I say let's evolve"—is spoken in the context of moving *beyond* ownership. Surely Tyler's sense of evolution as devolution flows from his view that human life is most meaningful when it is informed by the fundamental entropy of the universe.

"Listen up, maggots." Tyler speaks words of discouragement through a megaphone. "You are not special. You are not a beautiful or unique snowflake. You are the same decaying organic matter as everything else. We are the all-singing, all-dancing crap of the world. We are all part of the same compost heap." This statement is definitely not Hegelian, but it does have a physical monistic ring to it, akin to Marx's materialist notions of human composition. But while *Fight Club* displays a possible philosophical difference with basic Hegelian principles, it does bear a number of striking similarities to that illegitimate child of Hegelian thought, anarchism.

Anarchism and the *Fight Club* Philosophy

Congruent with and inspired by the Marxists, but fundamentally disagreeing with Marx, anarchists believe that Marx's proletariat uprising would not fundamentally alter the oppressive capitalist system, but would merely replace the current oppressors with similar oppressors in the future. In the 1890s, anarchist movements

---

*Interestingly, while Tyler himself rejects the notion of progress, it seems that Jack's thought runs along the dialectic described in Hegel's *Philosophy of Right*. Jack moves out of his basest particularity (unexamined desires for "versatile solutions for modern living") to universal reflection (Tyler's far-reaching views on the nature of property and reality) and on to a synthesized view (which rejects materialism but stops short of nihilism, making room for a genuine relationship with Marla).

cropped up mainly in France and Spain, but also in Britain and the United States. Even though the general climate of fear produced a widely held international conspiracy theory that the western European states would be overthrown by violence, the acts of terror during this time were sporadic and unorganized. The 1960s and 1970s witnessed more anarchist activity, this time concentrated in Germany and Italy, but again not leaving Britain and America unscathed.*

Like anarchism, Tyler's is a working man's movement. To the police commissioner, Tyler says, "Look. The people you are after are the people you depend on. We cook your meals. We haul your trash. . . . We guard you while you sleep. Do not fuck with us." The fight club truly does not discriminate based on race, religion, or socioeconomic status. As Tyler finishes smacking a guy from jaw to pavement, a corporate type steps up and asks, "Can I be next?" "All right, man. Lose the tie," is Tyler's response.

Anarchism is fundamentally an anti-authoritarian movement. In contradistinction to Marxism's *exchange* of capitalist central authorities for proletariat ones, the anarchists seek a completely decentralized, anti-state environment built on voluntary rather than compulsory relations. They oppose not just capitalism, but any imperialist or fascist state. They seek a more democratic type of law and rule. In the same way that anarchism questions the legitimacy of the state to govern affairs, so *Fight Club* derides the unquestioning legitimacy of authority. The *Fight Club* DVD subversively follows the FBI copyright warning by splicing in a fake label that states: "Are you so impressed with authority that you give credence to all who claim it?" There is no central leader of fight club. At its height, no one took center stage except the two men fighting, while "the leader walked through the crowd, out in the darkness." Out of Lou's stale basement grow "tightly regimented cells capable of operating *independently of central leadership*" (italics added). Anarchists of the past often

---

*For an excellent overview of anarchism, see D. Miller, *Anarchism* (London: Dent, 1984).

attacked state officials, such as politicians, policemen, and judges, focusing their violence toward those at the top of industry and capitalism. In the same way, members of Project Mayhem terrorize Police Commissioner Jacobsen at a banquet by threatening to send each of his "family jewels" to both the *New York Times* and the *Los Angeles Times*, "press-release style."

Another form of this anti-authoritarianism is anarchism's atheism. Just as Marx believed religion was used to justify capitalist oppression and lull the masses into complacency, so too the anarchists became atheists for similar reasons. Tyler is not a full-fledged atheist, but he does have a low view of the Divine. While giving Jack a chemical burn, he preaches, "The first soap was made from the ashes of heroes, like the first monkey shot into space. Our fathers were our models for God. If our fathers bailed, what does that tell us about God? You have to consider the possibility that God does not like you. He never wanted you. In all probability, He hates you. . . . We are God's unwanted children? So be it!" In Tyler's theology, God is an absent father, too busy working in the corporate world to raise a son. If this understanding of Tyler's view of God is correct, it is much like the atheism found in Marxism and anarchism. Just like Marx's father rejected his Jewish heritage for Lutheranism because it was good for business, Tyler's atheism could stem from his father's/God's compromise with the corporate world.

Anarchists often used terror tactics and violence as their means of decentralization. Comparison with the chaos created by Project Mayhem in *Fight Club* is rightly made with terrorism. Jack describes Tyler as "*the* guerrilla terrorist of the food service industry." And when Jack—after realizing he is Tyler Durden—goes to turn himself in, he says, "I am the leader of a terrorist organization responsible for numerous acts of vandalism and assault all over the city." Some terrorist acts by anarchists were used in service of their larger agenda—robberies or kidnappings were considered justified because they were means of raising money. Like an anarchist subverting his oppressor in order to fund his activities, Jack blackmails his boss into keeping him on the payroll without coming to work. "We now had corporate sponsorship," Jack declares.

The most intriguing similarity between anarchism and *Fight Club* is their similar propaganda. It was anarchists who developed the concept and practice of "propaganda by the deed." Although some critics of anarchism tend to equate this with terrorism, it has a different purpose than terrorism and may or may not include direct violence against persons. While terrorism seeks to instill fear among the populace, often through killing, intentional deeds of propaganda seek to raise collective awareness. Anarchists also sometimes preferred to use dynamite for these activities. Often, the target of an anarchist's bomb would be something representative of the whole capitalist and/or fascist order, such as a café, boutique, or trendy store. These were public acts meant to arouse the revolutionary consciousness of laborers who, spending eleven or twelve hours per day working in a factory just to survive, had no time or energy to read socialist literature. Of course, anarchists did carry out assassinations of government officials and executions of land owners who were believed to be involved in the hierarchical oppression of the peasant masses. Because of this conflicted relationship with their governments, and in order for their propaganda to be effective, anarchists usually operated clandestinely.

Several comparisons can be made here. Tyler's program of terror is not best compared with Nietzsche's nihilism (contra Edward Norton's DVD commentary). The acts in *Fight Club* are not senseless; they have a purpose. Tyler's method is "propaganda by the deed." These acts begin innocently enough, like "splicing single frames of pornography into family films." But they soon become much more public. Operation Latte Thunder is designed not only to "destroy a piece of corporate art" and "trash a franchise coffee bar," but also makes the general public aware of the evils inherent in these icons. The homework assignments Tyler gives the members of fight club function in the same way. They destroy television antennas and demagnetize rental movies to wake people from the stultifying effects of the media. They awaken people to the sins of the auto industry by exposing its polluting effects via a billboard, reversing the tire spikes at a car garage, smashing in the headlights of fancy cars (especially the designer VW Bug), and feeding pigeons atop a

BMW car dealership. To raise awareness about the evils of airline corporations, they replace the emergency cards in airplane seat backs with more realistic ones.* Other public deeds of propaganda around the city are found among Tyler's newspaper clippings, such as the cutting of power at a local mall, the befouling of a fountain, and the shaving of monkeys (presumably in mockery of NASA's shaven space monkeys). Finally, monitors from a retail computer store are sent, ablaze, out the front window. These acts are not merely "random acts of violence" meant to financially frustrate corporations, nor can they be defined as narrowly as "terrorism." They are public events produced by a clandestine group, intended to arouse the social consciousness of the masses that are both oppressed by and participate in corporate exploitation.

Another good example of extreme propaganda by the deed is the "human sacrifice" scene. Tyler's holding a gun to the convenience store clerk's head is meant to raise his consciousness and—by retaining his driver's license—to keep it raised. It is meant to "scare him to *life*." The human sacrifices of ancient heroes was what created soap. This human sacrifice was meant to make him into a hero and get him out of working in his mundane, meaningless job that is wasting his potential. Later in the movie, on the back of the door to Tyler's room, we see dozens of driver's licenses hanging with pride.

Just as anarchists use explosives such as dynamite in their deeds of propaganda, so the members of fight club do not hesitate to use such weaponry. It is dynamite that blows up Jack's apartment. The "act of vandalism" broadcast on the evening news is a four-alarm fire at the Parker-Morris building. This is the grandest deed of propaganda Project Mayhem has accomplished so far in the film: They paint a smiley face on the side of the high-rise in neon green, and use two offices as flaming eyeballs. The movie's end, narrated at the

---

*Depicted on the pamphlets are various images, including a father fighting another passenger for an oxygen mask and then stiff-arming his son to guard it, a guy praying next to a woman who is flying out a door in midair, and dead people—all amidst smoke and flames.

beginning, culminates in "the demolitions committee of Project Mayhem [wrapping] the foundation columns of a dozen buildings with blasting gel."

The irony of anarchism is that it employs violent means to achieve a peaceful end. This has been the enduring criticism of those who study anarchism. Tyler's project has a similar ethic. Despite all his anarchy, he has respect for human life. The car accident that Tyler causes is actually a humanizing event. Jack finally has compassion for those affected by such accidents rather than just seeing them as a statistic. Tyler's interpretation: "We just had a near-life experience!" When his good friend Robert Paulson is shot, leaving his head like a raw piece of bloody meat loaf, Tyler reverts to being Jack—his safe, sensible self. The gun he uses to scare the convenience store clerk into self-actuality is, in fact, empty. Tyler is the one willing to save "infectious human waste," in contrast to Jack, who wishes Marla would have died. We only hear second-hand that Chloe has passed away. When Jack protests Tyler murdering people by blowing up the credit card buildings, Tyler ensures him that the buildings are completely empty. "We're not killing anyone, man. We're setting them free!" Even Jack himself survives a would-be fatal handgun blast in the mouth so that only his "imaginary friend" dies. (Admittedly, the violence in *Fight Club* is somewhat idealized, with minimal collateral damage to humans.) So while our hero may enjoy primal, fist-smacking, blood-splattering fights, he certainly has an aversion to actual death and killing. In fact, the most gruesome portrayal of death comes at the hands of corporate greed—the skin of the auto-industry victim seared to a vinyl seat.

The goal of anarchists is not nihilism, but financial equity. In Italy, anarchists moved from town to town, liberating debtors by burning the financial archives, distributing tax receipts, and destroying mechanisms the state used to observe and collect surplus goods (like counters on grain machines). They would then distribute weapons to the peasants and incite social brigandage. Not unlike modern reactions to *Fight Club*, some people applauded the efforts of these anarchists while others found them horrible.

Tyler's Ultimate Economic Vision

"Why was Tyler building an army?" Jack wonders. "To what greater purpose? To what greater good?" The endgame is to blow up the buildings of ten major credit card companies as well as the TRW building. Their reasoning—much like that of Solon and Nehemiah in ancient times—is: "If you erase the debt record, then we all go back to zero." "Out of these windows," Tyler says during the count-down to the explosions, "we will view the collapse of financial history. One step closer to economic equilibrium." (The prophetic nature of this 1999 film, with respect to the terrorist attacks of 9/11, is chilling.) While corporations ramp up to colonize deep space and department stores are charging insane amounts for Tyler's soap, he has a different agenda. "In the world I see," Tyler tells Jack in a dreamlike sequence, "you're stalking elk through the Grand Canyon forests around the ruins of Rockefeller Center. You'll wear leather clothes that will last you the rest of your life. You'll climb the thick kudzu vines that wrap the Sears Tower. And when you look down, you'll see tiny figures pounding corn, laying strips of venison in the empty carpool lane of some abandoned superhighway." Tyler's aim is much like an anarchist vision of utopia. No government, no technology, no material possessions—everything is decentralized.

The great schizophrenic irony of the film's ending is that Tyler dies at the hands of his corporate counterpart, Jack. The movie is then completed, in calm climax, with the implosion of the city's major financial buildings. "Economic equilibrium" is now a more attainable goal, and Tyler is dead. But this is in keeping with the spirit of Tyler Durden. As with the anarchist uprisings that were inevitably suppressed by various governments, the liberation of indebted "slaves" and the heightening of social consciousness is accomplished nonetheless. One even senses a martyrdom ideology in the film as Tyler dies seconds before the liberating corporate collapse.

The similarities between anarchism and *Fight Club*'s philosophy are remarkable. Both arise among the working-class poor and rage against capitalism and the authorities that promote them. The anarchists and members of Project Mayhem use both propaganda by the deed (and dynamite) to awaken the social consciousness of the masses. Most importantly, they are both reacting to a gross financial imbalance resulting in the oppressive enslavement of the masses by their current power structure. And they both live by the socialist principle: "On a long enough timeline, the survival rate for everyone drops to zero."

James Corbett lives in Japan where he runs The Corbett Report Web site. He is currently working on a documentary entitled *Film, Literature and the New World Order.*

Soap and Anarchy
A BARTHESIAN READING OF FIGHT CLUB
James Corbett

I f particularly perceptive marketing can give insight into a film, then what are we to make of the marketing of *Fight Club*? One of the first emblematic images of the film is to be found on the movie poster or DVD cover, a photograph of a vibrantly pink, slightly foamy bar of soap, bristling with the words FIGHT CLUB, as if it were a brand. Visitors to the film's official Web site are treated to a flash animation proclaiming, "Tyler has a vision. Tyler has something to say. Tyler makes soap." The Web site's main navigation page bears the tagline "Mischief. Mayhem. Soap." Soap, it would seem, is not something incidental to the meaning of the film. What role, then, does soap play in helping us understand the film's action?

In order to understand the importance of soap in *Fight Club*, we must look to French critic and philosopher Roland Barthes' essay, "Soap-powders and Detergents," published in French in 1957 in a collection entitled *Mythologies*. In this essay, Barthes examines the advertising campaigns of the then-burgeoning soap industry of 1950s France. Dividing cleaning agents into the broad categories of "chlorinated fluids" and "soap-powders," Barthes finds very different iconography in their marketing. Advertising for chlorinated fluids "rests on the idea of a violent, abrasive modification of matter: the connotations are of a chemical or mutilating type: the product 'kills' the dirt." On the other hand, soap-powders "are separating agents: their ideal role is to liberate the object from its circumstantial imperfection: dirt is 'forced out' and no longer killed." These two very different mythologies of cleaning agents—the cleansing fire vs. the separating agent—provide insight into the social, spiritual, economic, and, ultimately, revolutionary philosophy of *Fight Club*.

I

Personal hygiene, closely linked with the idea of beauty, is a social construction that regulates the behavior of a society. Since the advent of modern science and the realization of the correlation between cleanliness and health, hygiene and beauty have been intimately linked in the popular imagination. Regular washing of clothes and bodies with soap is a relatively recent phenomenon, but one that the public has by and large accepted and internalized. The idea of cleanliness as an inherent good extends from the working world, where employees are expected to dress "professionally" in neatly pressed white shirts, to the most intimate relationships, where lovers are reminded by advertisers of the importance of white teeth and minty-fresh breath. These ideas are enforced from within by our sense of vanity and from without by social pressures that encourage conformity to the ideal of cleanliness.

Soap advertisers, for their part, take advantage of these popular conceptions by appealing, as Barthes points out, directly to our sense of "vanity, a social concern with appearances, by offering for comparison two objects, one of which is *whiter than* the other" (emphasis in the original). This strain of advertising survives virtually unchanged today, perhaps best exemplified by the ubiquitous and viciously circular "whiter than white" advertising for laundry soaps. Here, cleanliness, represented by an idealized "whiteness," is presented as something inherently good. Advertising manifests this ideal whiteness and cleanliness in the unrealistically "beautiful" models that are presented as the ideal aim of hygiene. In *Fight Club*, the narrator sneers at a Gucci underwear advertisement on a bus showing an improbably muscular, unblemished body, decapitated by the positioning of a handrail in the frame, sporting a glossy pair of black briefs. "Is that what a man's supposed to look like?" he asks Tyler Durden, provoking an ironic snort. Even Dove's recent "Campaign for Real Beauty," in which models with certain physical traits previously avoided by advertisers (like freckles and potbellies) are presented as "really" beautiful, plays into the pervading norm by continuing to equate this beauty with the use of cleaning agents. Given such a context, it is easy to see how Tyler's proclamation that he doesn't "want to die without any scars" already smacks of the revolutionary.

The social controls that rebuke such a revolutionary attitude are already inherent in soap advertising, however. Seen in its role as a separating agent, sorting dirt from pure whiteness, soap's "function is keeping public order, not making war." In the advertising for Omo, a brand of soap popular at the time Barthes wrote his essay, for instance, "dirt is a diminutive enemy, stunted and black, which takes to its heels from the fine immaculate linen at the sole threat of the judgement of *Omo*." This image is reminiscent of the narrator's boss, who, exasperated by the narrator's increasingly disheveled appearance at work—shirt half untucked, necktie tied too short by half, blood stains dirtying his clothes—tells him to "Take the rest of the day off, come back Monday with some clean clothes. . . . Get yourself together." Here, the boss's social role of "keeping public order" comes up against the fight club's aesthetic of "making war," in which appearance is not based on an idealized whiteness, but on utility for fighting. "Fight club," as the narrator says, "became the reason to cut your hair short or trim your fingernails."

The fight club and Project Mayhem, its anarcho-revolutionary offshoot, revel in their own dirtiness. At one point shortly after the founding of fight club, when the narrator is brushing his teeth—an image shown multiple times throughout the film, and always involving a fair bit of foam frothing from his mouth—he shakes out a loose tooth and stares at it in disbelief. Tyler remarks, "Hey, even the *Mona Lisa* is falling apart." Here, Tyler effectively gives the lie to the idea of cleanliness as beauty by pointing out that perhaps the most iconic image of Western art, and a byword for an ideal of aesthetic beauty, is itself faded, blemished, and decaying. Later Tyler refers to Project Mayhem's members as "maggots," and uses a loudspeaker to intone to the recruits, "You are the same decaying organic matter as everything else." In this formulation, life itself is equated with an inherent dirtiness, being compared to "crap" and collectively called a "compost heap."

This attitude, going against the norms of society, makes the fight club itself into a sort of dirt to be attacked by the separating agents of society: bosses, bar owners, and crusading police commissioners alike. When the owner of Lou's Tavern attempts to "clean up" his premises by getting rid of the unauthorized fight club in the bar's basement, he uses violence to attempt to remove the offending "dirt." Tyler, however, attacks the owner simply by dirtying him with his own blood. In an effort to escape the filthy scene, Lou agrees to let the fight club continue.

Typically, the narrator figures the conflict between society's idealized cleanliness and the fight club's embrace of dirtiness as a type of fight, one in which the dirty fight club will not "take to its heels" at the threat of judgment. "I got right in everyone's hostile little face," he says in voiceover. "Yes, these are bruises from fighting. Yes, I'm comfortable with that," he affirms. From this proclamation to his following assertion, "I am enlightened," seems quite a jump in logic. But this points to the second aspect of soap's importance in the film, that of spirituality.

II

Cleanliness is next to godliness, according to conventional wisdom. And if cleanliness is associated with the good and dirtiness with evil, then it is not a great leap from this to construct a mythology of cleanliness as akin to spirituality. Again, this is reflected in soap advertising. Here, the soap threatens "judgement [sic]" on the cowardly dirt, taking on a messianic role. Soap as separating agent helps "liberate" an inherently clean substance from the invading dirt. As Barthes points out, "matter here is endowed with value-bearing states."

Tyler Durden's spirituality of soap bears in its messianic role a violent repudiation of evil. The mythology here is not that of soap as a separating agent but as a cleansing fire. This is brought to the fore in his story of the discovery of soap. According to Tyler, "Ancient peoples found that their clothes got cleaner when they washed them at certain points in the river" because "human sacrifices were once made on the hills above this river." This account of soap's bloody history is fairly common, echoed, for instance, on the Web site of the Soap and Detergent Association (an organization remarkable, perhaps, only for the fact that it exists). Their version of the story, accompanied by illustrations vaguely reminiscent of the emergency landing illustrations that Tyler mocks on the airplane during his first meeting with the narrator, runs thusly: "Soap got its name, according to an ancient Roman legend, from Mount Sapo, where animals were sacrificed. Rain washed a mixture of melted animal fat, or tallow, and wood ashes down into the clay soil along the Tiber River. Women found that this clay mixture made their wash cleaner with much less effort."

Tyler's colorful account of soap's history is doubly fanciful. Firstly, the story of Mount Sapo itself, attributed only to an "ancient Roman legend," is, in the estimation of Wikipedia, "probably a hoax." And secondly, Tyler has taken the liberty of changing the story's account of "animal sacrifices" into "human sacrifices." This is not a trivial distinction. In making the tale into one of human sacrifice, Tyler anthropomorphizes the soap, proclaiming that "the first soap was made from the ashes of heroes." Here soap takes on the role of the wine in the Christian act of communion, the result of a chemical reaction akin to transubstantiation, which turns the blood of a savior into a substance that will cleanse us of evil.

Tyler's understanding of the cleansing fire thus casts soap as what Barthes terms an "absolute fire, a savior but a blind one." In this formulation, the cleaning agent is not good in a straightforward sense, as it will kill anything with which it comes into contact, good or evil, so long as it is weak. Soap's corrosive chemical components are experienced "as a sort of liquid fire, the action of which must be carefully estimated, otherwise the object itself would be affected, 'burnt.'" Perhaps unsurprisingly, then, baptism into Tyler's soap cult requires a chemical burn, a reminder of the dangerous, corrosive nature of salvation itself.

The spirituality of the fight club is the spirituality of violence, in which the body is literally brutalized in order to remove the stains on the soul. The fight club, we are told by the narrator, "wasn't about winning or losing," but is instead compared to a "Pentecostal church" after which "we all felt saved." Project Mayhem begins when new recruits are forced to wait outside with all their belongings for three days, like those wishing to join a Buddhist monastery. Tyler and the narrator seek to sanctify violence almost as some religious sects glorify self-flagellation. According to this theory, it is only through violence and suffering that we can understand the cleansing fire of salvation.

As the narrator is writhing under the pain of the chemical burn, Tyler explains that "Our fathers were our models for God." It would not be too far off the mark to suggest that he may as well have said, "Soap is our model for God." Soap as the cleansing fire is indeed Tyler's model for a god of vengeance and a spirituality of violence.

To be sure, it is a long and fanciful road from the social nicety of the separating agent to the fiery vengeance of the cleansing fire. The former mythology glorifies outward beauty as an ideal, the latter glorifies the scarred, bruised body. One reflects a belief in the body as inherently clean and in need of a separation from outward dirt, the other sees the body as inherently dirty and in need of violent salvation. How, then, are we to reconcile these two vastly different metaphorical understandings of soap?

III

Barthes himself deflates his own rather fanciful argument of soap as "separating agent" and "cleansing fire" with one final quotidian fact that even the most hardened of realists would not begrudge: "There is one plane on which *Persil* [soap-powder] and *Omo* [detergent] are one and the same," he asserts, "the plane of the Anglo-Dutch trust [soap brand] *Unilever*" (emphasis in the original). That is to say, regardless of the mythology constructed to understand it, soap is now nothing more than a commodity. While the first soap may have been "made from the ashes of heroes," now it is made in factories from industrially produced chemicals. Entering the world of the commodity, soap is sold not merely as a cleaning agent, but as a luxury item.

Following the old adage, "Sell the sizzle, not the steak," soap marketers often sell not the soap but the foam, appealing to an understanding of bubbles as extravagance. More specifically, Barthes notes that foam signifies luxury in that it "appears to lack any usefulness" and "its abundant, easy, almost infinite proliferation allows one to suppose there is in the substance from which it issues a vigorous germ, a healthy and powerful essence." This in part explains the effectiveness of the image on the cover of *Fight Club*. The implied violence of the *Fight Club* brand is seen oozing out of the bar of soap in the form of bubbles, a type of proliferation that threatens to cover all that it comes into contact with in its own particular essence.

Tellingly, Barthes figures the iconic marketing image of this foamy decadence as the "film star in her bath." Indeed, there is something inherently sexual in the way soap bubbles titillate by simultaneously hiding and revealing the naked body. In the narrator's case, the titillating obscurity of foam is not experienced as a pleasure, but as a poor substitute for his own lack of love life. This is reflected in close-ups of the narrator foaming from the mouth as he brushes his teeth vigorously, in evident sexual frustration, while listening to Tyler and Marla coupling. The image is repeated as we see him scrubbing his shirt with a toothbrush in the sink, eliciting a meager amount of foam as the walls shake from the amorous activities upstairs. The froth of the soap acts as a kind of stand-in for sex, and the vigorous motion of scrubbing becomes the next best thing to the act itself.

Like all successful businesses, the Paper Street Soap Co.—the economic arm of Tyler Durden's operation—understands the appeal of its product. The inherent appeal of anything handmade, the extravagance and sexuality offered by foamy soap, the promise of cleanliness and its attendant societal benefits; all these reasons help explain why department stores are willing to pay twenty dollars a bar for Tyler's soap. The fact that, by raiding the liposuction clinic for the raw material of their soap, they are in effect "selling rich women their own fat asses back to them" is an irony not lost on the narrator. Indeed, it is part of the subversion of fight club and Project Mayhem that they are only too willing to use the appeal of the commodity against the very people who so highly value material wealth. The proceeds from the Paper Street Soap Co. go directly into funding Project Mayhem's fight against "the basic assumptions of civilization, especially the importance of material possessions."

As a commodity, then, soap becomes a weapon against itself, a part of the fight against commodification. Here we reach perhaps the most important soap mythology of *Fight Club*: soap as a weapon of subversion.

IV

"You know, with enough soap one could blow up just about anything," Tyler tells the narrator as they prepare to render the stolen fat from the liposuction clinic. Glycerin, it turns out, is a key byproduct of the soap-making process, separating from the tallow as it hardens. Usually this glycerin is stirred back into the mixture, thus making a glycerin soap. As Tyler points out, however, this layer of glycerin can be skimmed off and used for an altogether different purpose. Through a process not all that much more complicated than a typical high school chemistry project, soap-making leads to bomb-making. Violence, it seems, is encoded into the very chemistry of soap.

The appeal of soap for Tyler Durden, then, is manifold. Not only is it a source of revenue, not only does it provide a model for a spirituality based on fiery salvation, it is in fact a weapon, the instrument of violence through which he seeks to spread his own particular social philosophy throughout the world. What this social philosophy might be is never explicitly defined, but it is articulated several times in reference to what it is not. It is not, for instance, ascribing importance to material possessions. It involves a theory of identity in which people are defined only by what they are not: their jobs, their money, their cars, the contents of their wallets, their khakis. It has as its teleology not some utopian ideal but a post-apocalyptic scene of abandoned highways and buildings overgrown with vines. When confronted by the narrator about the purpose of Project Mayhem, Tyler descends into trite clichés such as "We're not killing anyone, man, we're setting them free!" and "You wanna make an omelette, you gotta break some eggs." Tyler's agenda, it turns out, is not nearly so important as the method he uses to achieve it.

Violence being a central characteristic of both fight club and Project Mayhem, the anarcho-revolutionary spirit of Tyler's scheme is reflected in soap, which is, by a few alchemical steps, the physical instantiation of the cleansing fire that he sees as a type of salvation. In this case, the bombs planted at various buildings around the city are meant to destroy the credit record, thereby theoretically putting everyone on the same economic playing field. Whatever one makes of the likelihood of such a scheme, it is at least in keeping with the explosive power of soap to change society. As Barthes puts it, soap creates "a large surface of effects out of a small volume of causes." Tyler seeks to unlock this violent potential from a society based on social order, which has "disguised the abrasive function of the detergent under the delicious image of a substance at once deep and airy which can govern the molecular order of the material without damaging it."

Taking our cue from Barthes, we find the mythology of a substance embedded in that substance's advertising. Here, then, we are vindicated in taking the bar of soap on the DVD cover as the film's iconic image. Soap, recognized instantly as a commodity, is subverted by the *Fight Club* brand, which threatens to spread its own violent spirituality in a frothy foam.

Works Cited

Barthes, Roland. "Soap-powders and Detergents" in *Mythologies*. New York: Farrar, Straus & Giroux, 1998.
Fight Club Official Web site. <www.foxmovies.com/fightclub>
The Soap and Detergent Association Web site. "History." <www.cleaning101.com/cleaning/history>
Wikipedia. "Soap." http://en.wikipedia.org/wiki/Soap>

Ned Vizzini is the author of three books, including *Be More Chill,* about a supercomputer in pill form that delivers advice like Tyler Durden.

Tyler Durden, Boss Playa

Ned Vizzini

olin Powell says that we always know what the right decision is. We can agonize, analyze, and debate the options that life presents us every day, but deep down we know how to act in all situations; we simply get scared of what is correct.

Of course, Mr. Powell says this with reference to noble, moral decisions. *Fight Club* takes the same stance on base human instincts.

Tyler Durden always knows what to do. He is exciting, free, and fearless. While his choices are often reprehensible, they are always correct within the context of our nameless narrator's life. Without Tyler, Edward Norton's everyman is as useless as Hamlet, slinking through his years, waiting for death.

With Tyler, he's a legend.

But Tyler's advice is nothing special. It's what our Everyman already knows to be true: It's a *good idea* to build a cult, make bombs, and screw the hell out of Helena Bonham Carter.

Tyler just makes it easier to see.

Because there's no question: We don't just know what the right thing to do is in our lives. We know what the *wrong* thing to do is, and the *fun* thing to do, and the brave thing to do, and the legendary thing. Go and get a job or go and start a cult—isn't it obvious what the answer is there? It's wrong to start a cult, but it's also fun, and brave, and legendary. And Tyler flips everything around, makes it good as well. Moral relativism is a necessary part of any fight, because one side's bad, and one side's good, but the other side thinks the other way. You get away with everything being good *and* bad when Tyler's on your side.

And then, of course, there's the sexy thing to do. Say what you want about the rest of *Fight Club,* if we always listened to Tyler about sex, filtered out the fighting, and let in the assuredness, we'd have a pretty creative and promiscuous society, something like the '60s: a world of fearless pick-up artists, freed from their trepidation at bars and parties and able to act with impunity. Those moral relativists— very slick operators.

Tyler is the ultimate wingman. With him on our side, no conquest is out of reach. He's the dark side of Colin Powell, the person who always knows what's right to do, even if what you want to do is very, very wrong.

Christian McKinney, with the approval and assistance of his advisor Janet Kinch, organized the first (2001) and second (2003) Chuck Palahniuk conferences while an undergraduate at the University of Edinboro, Pennsylvania. This paper was first presented at "How We Learn: Technologies in English Studies," the English Association of Pennsylvania State Universities' Annual Conference, October 26, 2000, East Stroudsburg University of Pennsylvania.

The Salvation Myth

HUMAN RELATIONSHIPS TO TECHNOLOGY IN *FIGHT CLUB*

Christian McKinney

Introduction/Thesis

Among Western and Occidental societies in the late twentieth century, the term "technoculture" has entered both corporate and cultural lexicons. In an age of globalization where other terms such as "information technology" and "knowledge economy" are common in locales as far distant from Western culture as China, this fusion of "technology" and "culture" may seem to be an appropriate addition to language. "Technoculture," however, despite the novelty of the word, is something of a misnomer. All human societies, even the most ancient, are technocultures in the sense that members utilize and work with technology and tools to alter the natural condition of their environments. Technology by itself is nothing but an abstract idea until someone attempts to apply it in a causal relationship in the material world. This distinction between the abstract and the application of technology is crucial to understanding human relationships to it. For the purposes of this study, a working redefinition can be found in Richard Merelman's article on postmodernism and liberalism. Merelman, a professor of political science at the University of Wisconsin–Madison, states, "The culture of technology is simply the structure of feeling that technology helps to create between society and the self." Human beings, then, have ideas of technology, some of which are applied materially and thus causally alter the natural world. The alteration of the natural world influences not only cultural values, as Arnold Pacey notes in his book *The Culture of Technology*, but also the conceptualization of new technology. The result is a circular process of abstraction, application, and interaction.

Humanity's circular interaction with technology is an integral theme of *Fight Club*, both in Palahniuk's 1996 novel and the 1999 film adaptation by screenwriter Jim Uhls and director David Fincher. Though the film adaptation and the novel are at points markedly different in terms of plot, the narrative structures, protagonist characterizations, and driving impetus behind both stories are utterly parallel. As such, *Fight Club* relates the development of an unnamed narrator from a desperate young American professional who feels trapped in a world of work and consumerism to a self-styled messianic figure and demagogue of apocalyptic proportions. The protagonists of both stories, furthermore, develop a fanatical hatred of Westernized cultural values and the perceptions of technology produced by postmodern American society. In the protagonists' view, American society is dominated not by the comfortable, futuristic world implied by "technoculture," but rather by what can be referred to as the "myth of salvation," a misplaced and false trust in the ability of technology to save humanity from itself. The members of American society, in the opinions of Palahniuk and the makers of the film, strive to find comfort, happiness, and ultimately redemption simply by accruing new and fashionable applied technologies. The result is a world with no meaning where, as one character says in the film, "everything is falling apart." The protagonists, therefore, work diligently to destroy American consumer and corporate culture with extreme pranks and acts of terrorism in an attempt to reset both ethical and material values to hunter-gatherer levels. Such regression, in the protagonists' view, is the only means of escaping the faulty, culture-wide mythology of salvation through technology. Rather than save humanity, technology has already destroyed it by warping its cultural priorities while simultaneously rendering the earth increasingly uninhabitable. Implicit, therefore, in the driving philosophy behind the protagonists, who form an army of anti-culture warriors known as Project Mayhem, is the idea that applied technology is only valid and fit for human use if it is accompanied by a value-equivalent sacrifice. An analysis of the novel and the film will demonstrate how the clash between the concepts of salvation and heroic sacrifice relate as a conflict of diametric ideologies symbolized by human interaction with technology and the culture that results from it.

Summary/Analysis of *Fight Club*

In both versions of *Fight Club*, the narrator (played by Edward Norton in the film) is an insomniac who becomes addicted to joining support groups for terminal or crippling diseases he does not have, in order to experience life at its worst and escape the fake holism of material success. He realizes that life "comes down to nothing," and that crying at support groups actually cures his insomnia. The act of pretending to be dying liberates the narrator from the emptiness of his job as a recall coordinator at a major automobile corporation, and from the cold sterility of his fashionably furnished condo, which in turn allows him to sleep. The narrator's sense of life is renewed after each meeting, and consequently he says of the experience in the novel:

> Walking home after a support group, I felt more alive than I'd ever felt. I wasn't host to cancer or blood parasites; I was the little warm center that the life of the world crowded around.
> And I slept. Babies don't sleep this well.
> Every evening, I died, and every evening, I was born.
> Resurrected.

The narrator is eventually forced to divvy up his support groups with Marla Singer (played by Helena Bonham Carter in the film), a fellow disease-faking "tourist" who attends the meetings out of a bored, morbid fascination with suffering, combined with her own desperate search for empathy. The presence of another tourist, however, prevents the narrator from crying and hence negates the "cure" for his insomnia. Not being able to cry, the narrator says, keeps him from "hitting bottom," which he believes is requisite for salvation.

The intrusion of Singer into his world of support groups refuels the narrator's sense of material entrapment that explodes into terrorist action later in the story. In both the novel and the film, the narrator accuses Singer of "ruining everything."

The narrator, furthermore, first expresses his sense of entrapment when he outlines the circumstances of his job and the furnishings of his home, a condo he describes as a "filing cabinet for widows and young professionals." As for his domestic life, the narrator says, "Like so many others, I had become a slave to the IKEA nesting instinct. We used to read pornography. . . . Now it was the Horchow collection." In a sequence that Jonathan Romney, in the *New Statesman*, describes as one of the most brilliant parts of the film, the narrator's condo becomes a walk-through IKEA catalog as descriptions, prices, and ordering information appear on the screen next to the narrator's furniture. The narrator also says, in all seriousness, "I'd flip through catalogs and wonder, 'What kind of dining set defines me as a person?'" His early obsession with garnering the material symbols of wealth and success triggers a deep-seated sense of frustration and self-hatred that ultimately mushrooms into the main psychological thrust of the film.

The narrator, who is now addicted to support groups and is growing increasingly disillusioned with his old lifestyle, meets Tyler Durden (played by Brad Pitt in the film), a charismatic waiter, film projectionist, and soap manufacturer. The narrator encounters Durden while on a flight home from a business trip in the film adaptation, and in the novel they meet while he is on vacation. In Durden the narrator immediately discovers the living embodiment of every physical and mental characteristic he has ever lacked. Durden's maniacal pranks (he splices single frames of pornography into family films and urinates in the food he serves) appeal to the narrator's own hatred of culturally expected safety and convenience. (The narrator, for example, prays for a crash every time he's on a plane.) The narrator is drawn to Durden's athletic build, witty intelligence, and scathing sense of humor, and Durden quickly becomes the narrator's friend, guide, and father figure.

The narrator moves in with Durden after his condo mysteriously explodes while he is on a business trip. He calls Durden from a pay phone as he watches the fire department root through the smoldering debris of his old home, and the two agree to meet at a bar, where the narrator, after mournfully listing the contents of his devastated condo, tells Durden he was close to being "complete." Durden, after listening to the narrator's plight, outlines his own philosophy and initiates the first explicitly anti-consumerist dialogue in the story. In the film, Durden asks the narrator:

> "What are we, then?"
>
> "I don't know, consumers?"
>
> "Right. We are consumers. We are byproducts of a lifestyle obsession. Murder, crime, poverty—these things don't concern me. What concerns me is celebrity magazines, television with five hundred channels, some guy's name on my underwear. Rogaine, Viagra, Olestra. . . . I say, 'Never be complete.' I say, 'Let's evolve and let the chips fall where they may.'. . . The things you own end up owning you."

Once outside the bar, Durden agrees to let the narrator move in with him, but then asks the narrator for an extraordinary favor: "I want you to hit me as hard as you can. . . . I don't want to die without any scars." The narrator, taken aback and flustered at first, finally punches Durden, who almost immediately punches the narrator in return. The two beat each other to a pulp and are so liberated by the experience the narrator says, "We should do this again sometime."

After moving into Durden's home, a massive abandoned house the narrator describes as being in "the toxic waste part of town," Durden and the narrator start fight club, a male-only organization where men fight each other one on one simply for the intense physical rush of hand-to-hand combat, and for the experience of pain to circumvent the emotional numbness of their daily lives. The obsession with fight club develops into an all-consuming passion for its members; as the narrator says in the film, "Fight club became the reason to cut your hair short or trim your fingernails."

The narrator's initial euphoria in fight club and his idealized father-son relationship with Durden, however, is compromised when Durden saves Marla Singer's life after she overdoses on the popular anti-anxiety drug Xanax. Durden and Singer, drawn by each other's nihilistic sense of self-destruction, start an intensely violent sexual relationship that leaves the narrator feeling rejected and reminiscent of his childhood relationship with his parents.

Meanwhile, Durden's third job, soap manufacturing, involves stealing liposuctioned human fat—which Durden explains has an ideal salt balance for soap—from medical waste dumps and boiling it for the tallow. Durden also describes, in considerable detail, how the layer of glycerin that develops on the surface of the tallow can be mixed with other chemicals to create nitroglycerin and dynamite. "With enough soap," Durden says, "you could blow up just about anything." True to form, Durden sells his soap at twenty dollars a bar to upscale department stores, causing the narrator to remark, "We were selling rich women's fat asses back to them."

The narrator's sense of rejection, meanwhile, is worsened when Durden forms Project Mayhem, a quasimilitaristic pranks and misinformation front comprised of the more ardent members of fight club. The members of Project Mayhem move in with the narrator and Durden, turning the house into a self-sustaining headquarters where they plot the downfall of Western civilization. While Project Mayhem's subsequent terrorist activities are concerned with material icons and not "traditional" terrorist targets such as political or popular figures, slain members of Project Mayhem are nonetheless regarded as martyrs, and Durden murders several enemies of Project Mayhem in the novel.

The story is supercharged with total rebellion when the members of Project Mayhem start a massive campaign that involves spray painting and setting fire to the façades of office buildings, destroying coffee bars and corporate art, blowing up retail store displays, erasing cassettes at video rentals with an electromagnet, vandalizing cars, reversing tire spikes in parking lots, defacing billboards, trashing television antennas, making excrement catapults, replacing airline safety cards with fake ones that depict people fighting for oxygen masks and planes crashing in flames, and more.

Durden's role during this time is increasingly that of a demagogue. At the start of each session of fight club he rouses member support with inspirational speeches that seethe with disillusionment aimed directly at the salvation myth.

> Man, I've seen in fight club the strongest and smartest men who've ever lived. I see all this potential, and I see it squandered. Goddamn it, an entire generation pumping gas, waiting tables, slaves with white collars. . . .We're the middle children of history, man; no purpose or place. We have no Great War, no Great Depression. Our Great War is a spiritual war. Our Great Depression . . . is our lives. We've all been raised by television to believe that one day we'd all be millionaires and movie gods and rock stars, but we won't, and we're slowly learning that fact, and we're very, very pissed off.

This anger is further emphasized at one point in the film when Durden turns and speaks directly to the camera. The film's sprocket holes appear to jump and warp the image of Brad Pitt's face as he snarls, "You are not your job. You are not how much money you have in the bank. You are not the car you drive. You are not the contents of your wallet. . . . You are the all-singing, all-dancing crap of the world."

As Project Mayhem approaches its climax and final actualization, tension increases between Durden and the narrator, eventually sparking several confrontations. The narrator accuses Durden of neglecting him and taking Project Mayhem too far. Durden tells the narrator to forget what he knows about their friendship. After the narrator is nearly killed when Durden, who is driving, crashes their car (in the novel, a mechanic almost crashes it), Durden leaves to set up chapters of Project Mayhem and fight club in other major cities. While Durden finds recruits for his spiritual war, the narrator wanders ghostlike around his house, drunk and largely ignored by the cadres of an increasingly regimented Project Mayhem. Senior members take up Durden's role in his absence, spouting bits of Durden's dogma while running new fight clubs and training incoming cadets.

In the film, Project Mayhem culminates with the controlled demolition of the headquarters of several major credit card companies across America, an act that will supposedly erase the debt record of the populace and create economic chaos. In the novel, the plan is to blow up a skyscraper so that, when it falls, it demolishes the museum of natural history across the street, destroying the relics of civilization. The narrator, meanwhile, slowly rises from a confused haze and recovers enough from the car crash to catch wind of Durden's plans and races across the country to stop him. It is during this feverish chase that the narrator discovers that he and Durden are in reality the same person: Durden is actually a manifestation of the narrator's personality that takes control while the narrator is sleeping. The impact of this realization devastates the narrator, who attempts to turn himself in to the police to protect the world from the other side of his personality. The police who question him, however, are also members of Project Mayhem, and they have already been given instructions by Durden for them to stop the narrator/himself if he interferes with the plans. The narrator manages to escape from the police station and runs to one of the targeted buildings to disarm the bomb, but is stopped by Durden, who beats the narrator senseless, then forces him to the top of the building at gunpoint.

The final confrontation between Durden and the narrator occurs, in both the novel and the film, just moments before the explosions are set to begin. The narrator, who finally comes to grips with the fact that Durden is a manifestation of his own self-destructive urges, mentally wrests the gun away from Durden and says (in the film), "I want you to really listen to me. My eyes are open," just before shooting himself in the face. The narrator survives with a ragged hole blown through his left cheek. Durden disappears, and the narrator's personality is unified. The narrator, who tried to reconcile with Singer just before turning himself in to the police, completes the story by taking her hand just as office towers start exploding in the distance.

Technology, the Salvation Myth, and Heroic Sacrifice

The anti-technological philosophies of Durden and his cohorts are explicit in the story during its anti-capitalist dialogue, but the importance of humanity's relationship to technology is a deeper underpinning that forms the impetus of Project Mayhem. Durden's spiritual war, in this sense, is a confrontation between the ideals of heroic sacrifice and the salvation myth.

In what is perhaps the most telling and most important sequence of the entire story, Durden explains that soap was discovered when an ancient culture found that their clothes got cleaner if they washed them at a specific point in the river. On a hill above that spot, Durden explains, the same people burned human sacrifices. The melted fat of the sacrifices mixed with lye that was formed from a solution of rain water and wood ash from the pyres. The combination created a thick discharge that made its way down the river in the form of soap. Durden is so enamored by this historical association of pain and human sacrifice with the act of cleansing that he says, because it led to the discovery of soap, "It was right to kill all those people." During this sequence, Durden deliberately burns the narrator's hand with a solution of lye. The narrator, in agony, attempts to utilize guided meditation techniques he learned in his support groups to control the pain. Durden recognizes what the narrator is doing and chides him, "This is the greatest moment of your life . . . and you're off somewhere missing it!" The importance of recognizing the uplifting value of sacrifice is even more explicit in the film when Durden says, "The first soap was made from the ashes of heroes, like the first monkey shot into space. Without pain, without sacrifice, we would have nothing."

The theme of heroic sacrifice is hardly new. Indeed, as famed mythologist Joseph Campbell asserts, the idea of heroic sacrifice is one of the oldest, most universal myths of human culture. The novel premise in *Fight Club*, however, is the myth-destroying nature of postmodern society. Merelman argues that, prior to the development of postmodern technology—which he identifies as starting with the proliferation of nuclear weapons and genetic science in the 1950s—modernist technologies fostered myths that replaced "ideological fanaticism" with an interactive, "scientifically calculated application of power." Postmodern society, however, has bastardized the interactive element to the point that most Americans do not relate to technology on an intrapersonal level. Members of Western society are forced to interact with technology to the point of utter dependence, but few understand how technology actually works. The closest relationships most humans in a postmodern society can achieve with the technological products they use are those that are vaguely defined as "user friendly."

In such an environment, humanity appears to have lost control of its ability to direct its own development and discover or deal with the concept of salvation. Peter Berger and Thomas Luckmann, in their seminal work *The Social Construction of Reality*, define this sense of loss as "reification," the perception of human-based phenomena as objective *things* outside of human control. In other words, reification is a description of the postmodern phenomenon of technology being viewed not as a tool for human use, but as a distinct entity that one must reconcile with or face destruction. People who have difficulty understanding and using computers, for example, will frequently ascribe all computers with malicious human personalities and will mutter phrases like, "Computer are taking over the world." One only has to look to the "insane" computer HAL in *2001: A Space Odyssey* or the robots of The Terminator and The Matrix series to see reification in film. Reification in postmodern society is engendered when most people find themselves at the mercy of machines they cannot fix, food they cannot grow or raise, clothes they cannot make, and so on. Survival in such circumstances is possible only when one learns to operate the countless and complex tools that have become required just to live. The effect of this scenario is twofold. In one respect, postmodern society has unhinged most cultural understanding of the individual human's place in the universe. Humans are no longer the children of God (or any gods), nor are they the directors of their own fates as the thinkers of the Enlightenment once believed. Rather, they are individual entities loosely bound by disintegrating concepts of family, church, and society. The myths that defined cultures and sustained societies for millennia, in other words, are so shattered that they no longer apply. In another respect, the desocializing nature of postmodern society prevents groups of people from coming together and understanding, on a cultural level, the nature, mechanics, and values of the tools and ideas they use to survive. Rather than a cooperative effort to imbue technological applications with any localized morality, capitalist-driven competition rules the day.

In this vision of postmodern society, the only organizations that survive are primarily corporate and governmental. However, Jerry Mander, a director of the Public Media Center organization and ardent opponent of corporate globalization, notes that while corporations are comprised of humans, they are inherently amoral. As such, culture is defined by entities that are driven by profit growth through homogenization, but not by cultural advancement. The temporal result of the dominance of corporate culture, Mander claims, is a world where "soon, everyplace will look and feel like everyplace else . . . there'll scarcely be a reason ever to leave home." Even proponents of globalization admit its homogenizing tendencies. Robert Holton, a sociology professor at Flinders University of South Australia, claims that the complexities of regional cultures will successfully prevent the bleak vision of a homogenized world, but nonetheless recognizes that globalized culture "exhibits high levels of convergence around market-driven capitalism." The mythology that results from a largely homogenized corporate culture is one that holds that consumerist, medical, and military technologies are the only means of spiritual fulfillment. The "truly happy" person, in this view, is the one who achieves upward mobility and garners the most material possessions. *Fight Club's* narrator, for instance, was the precise model of this image before his insomnia and the explosion of his condo. While lip service is still paid to deeper spiritual and cultural values, the wild success and popularity of "self-manipulation" through self-help programs, and "cosmetic alteration of the self" through plastic surgery and tattooing, suggests otherwise. Cultural introspection, however, is incapable of generating a viable society. In the film, Durden adroitly captures the postmodern sense of introversion and inverts it when he asserts, "Self-improvement is masturbation."

In a postmodern society where cultural myths are replaced with corporate-sponsored messages and mass communication, the individual is split across a growing gap between a social, public vision of the self and a private, intrapersonal vision. Pacey elaborates on this concept and notes that the absence of unified values creates the paradox of postmodern distrust of technology and the concurrent total dependence upon it. In *Fight Club*, this dichotomy is echoed on all levels of self-awareness, especially in terms of disjointed social values. While Berger and Luckmann argue for the psychological necessity of "habitualization" that can be found in the institution, Palahniuk argues that current societal modes of habitualization are inherently dangerous. In this respect, Palahniuk says he was influenced by the power-relationship theories of Michel Foucault:

> We really have no freedom about creating our identities, because we are trained to want what we want. What is it going to take to break out and establish some modicum of freedom, despite all the cultural training that's been our entire existence? It's about doing the things that are completely forbidden, that we are trained to not want to do.

Furthermore, reification, at its most extreme, is the total objectification of the human sphere of existence. The world that Palahniuk describes in *Fight Club*, therefore, can be viewed as one that is almost totally reified. Though culture and technology are still human products, the protagonists, especially Durden, see only objective constructs beyond their control. In the sense of the salvation myth, redemption through material gain is an object that can be hated, fought, and destroyed. Durden frequently refers to his plans, projects, and pranks in terms of freedom and liberation, but the "slaves" he attempts to liberate are the exact same people who support the corporations he so despises.

The resulting contradiction of Durden's personality is best seen in terms of political constructs. At one end of the spectrum, Durden is an extreme neo-Marxist working to bring about complete and utter parity among the working class, to the point that members of Project Mayhem are referred to only as "space monkeys" and have no identity outside of the collective. At the other extreme, Durden is an anarchist who is constantly working against, as Palahniuk notes, every cultivated value in corporate society. Durden is fascinated with and revels in the forbidden. In the film, Durden constantly reminds his "space monkeys" that none of them is "a beautiful or unique snowflake," while simultaneously trumpeting the power of the individual will and heroic sacrifice. The contradiction, however, is resolved through the way in which Durden's philosophy is applied. According to Steven Marcus, nineteenth-century author Matthew Arnold defines two types of anarchy in his work *Culture and Anarchy*. The first, "spiritual anarchy," is the result of laissez-faire economic forms and rampant religious sectarianism brought about by the rise of the Protestant church. The second, "social anarchy," is regarded as the teleological end of modern democracy. Durden, then, can be viewed as a spiritual Marxist and a social anarchist.

In his role as a spiritual Marxist, Durden looks to the mostly extinct traditions of the heroic, which is in turn found in the symbols of passage from one world to the next. As such, both fight club and Project Mayhem are full of initiation rites. Fight club, for example, requires first-time members to fight, while to be initiated into Project Mayhem members must prove their dedication by waiting on the front porch of Durden's house for three days without food, shelter, or encouragement. Furthermore, new Project Mayhem members shed their possessions and clothing, shave off their hair, burn group leaders' hands with lye, and so on. The result is that members are freed from associations with the old social order and brought wholly under Durden's dominion. In the film, the narrator also identifies the power of Durden's presence when he refers to Project Mayhem as "Planet Tyler."

What fuels Durden's obsession with the heroic is ultimately the sort of communal structure that is believed to have existed before the establishment of private property and government. In the film, Durden makes a remark to the narrator that is a veiled confession to blowing up his condo: "The liberator who has destroyed my property has realigned my perception." Durden goes on to encourage the narrator to "reject the basic assumption of civilization, especially the importance of material possessions." Durden, therefore, dreams of a pastoral utopia where small, independent communities share a complete and total mythological and values system that is centralized around the development and use of technology that all members can understand. This is a throwback to Merelman's argument that modernist society allowed for individual creative expression through the understanding and tinkering with technological inventions. In the novel, Durden describes this vision in messianic terms: "It's Project Mayhem that's going to save the world. A cultural ice age. A prematurely induced dark age. Project Mayhem will force humanity to go dormant or into remission long enough for the Earth to recover." Durden further explicates his ultimate goal:

> Like fight club does with clerks and box boys, Project Mayhem will break up civilization so we can make something better out of the world.
>
> Imagine . . . stalking elk past department store windows . . . you'll wear leather clothes that will last you the rest of your life, and you'll climb the wrist-thick kudzu vines that wrap the Sears Tower. Jack and the beanstalk, you'll climb up . . . and the air will be so clean you'll see tiny figures pounding corn and laying strips of venison to dry in the empty car-

> pool lane of an abandoned superhighway stretching
> eight lanes wide and August-hot for a thousand
> miles.

The key to achieving Durden's dream is not just simple revolution, but rather total social anarchy. Durden rejects the Hobbesian view that humans are dependent on government, and he seeks to abolish the state through the destruction of corporate culture and private property. Durden believes that social order will be reestablished through small, independent communities. Durden, therefore, would argue with liberal philosophers like John Locke, who believed that the state was a better alternative than anarchy. When viewed from a latter-day postapocalyptic scenario, Locke's fears are rooted in visions of neo-Darwinian conflict for physical supremacy among roving gangs of warring tribes. Although not explicitly stated in the novel or the film, Durden would likely counter the liberal view by pointing out that what is considered anarchy today functioned perfectly well for humans for millennia before the development of government. Liberalism, therefore, is still derived in part from the Hobbesian view of humanity. In this sense, Durden has completely reversed Hobbes's theory of humankind. Rather than the "brutish" nature of humans necessitating government, government actually causes humans to be brutish. The true aim of Durden's apocalyptic fantasies, then, is not the final destruction of technology, but rather the eradication of "civilized" history. Note that in the novel Durden's real target of destruction is a museum across the street from the building he plans to blow up. Durden's plan in the novel, in many respects, is misguided and simplistic. Vast amounts of recorded history will still exist, no matter how many museums Durden destroys, but the symbolic significance of the museum reveals Durden's understanding that his vision cannot be achieved unless history itself is erased. It is within this reversal of the Hobbesian dynamic that Durden's contradictions are fully unified. The triumph of social anarchy, in other words, would automatically generate spiritual Marxism, hence unifying both the self and humanity's relationship to the natural world.

Project Mayhem, as a social movement, is ultimately born from the schizophrenic dichotomy of the narrator's personality and his sense of self-loathing and frustration. As Eric Hoffer, author of *The True Believer*, notes, "The estrangement from the self, which is a precondition for both plasticity and conversion, almost always proceeds in an atmosphere of intense passion." The narrator is the quintessential figure of intrapersonal estrangement. Hoffer also argues that a fanatic is one with a "single-minded dedication" that actually represents someone who is "holding on for dear life." This is readily palpable in both the novel and the film in the narrator's desperate search for a father figure. Throughout the story the narrator obsesses about the absence of fathers in his life, to the point that he invents a father in the form of Tyler Durden. Durden, however, is a father figure only to the extent that he guides the narrator toward the discovery of characteristics he has always possessed but has never been able to actualize. The narrator, unable to fully realize his whole personality for most of the story, temporarily aborts the process when he rebels against Project Mayhem. The narrator's simultaneous adoration and revulsion of the Durden side of his personality only serves to stoke his self-hatred further, which is evident in his scapegoating of Marla Singer as a despoiler. The narrator, whose parents divorced when he was six, has shifted his own sense of guilt for the dissolution of his family by blaming his mother, a process that he reenacts with Durden and Singer. The fact that the narrator actually *is* Durden, furthermore, would be regarded by both Campbell and Sigmund Freud as a postmodern retelling of the Oedipus myth. The narrator harbors feelings for Singer, but is unable to fully realize those feelings until he is prepared to destroy Durden. When the characters of the narrator and Durden are viewed as one person, therefore, the narrator's self-hatred is born from his inability to maintain a stable family and his subsequent quest for meaning through the salvation myth. Durden's formation of Project Mayhem is an extension of the narrator's own fury, a culture-wide reenactment of the struggle within himself.

The psychological impetus behind the narrator's construction of Durden and the formation of Project Mayhem is important to understanding why the protagonists of *Fight Club* vent most of their rage on technology. At one point in the story the narrator describes how his biological father would marry a woman, sire children with her, then divorce and move on to another woman with whom he would repeat the process. Durden follows a similar pattern when he abandons the narrator to start new chapters of fight club and Project Mayhem. The narrator finally begins to make the connection when he says in the film, "I'm all alone. My father dumped me. Tyler dumped me." The "space monkeys" that Durden leaves behind can be viewed as the spiritual equivalent of the real-life half brothers the narrator will never see. It is also important to note here that while fight club is open to any males, the members are predominately drawn from the same social pool where the narrator existed at the beginning of the film. Durden refers to them as "a generation of men raised by women," and describes them again as "slaves with white collars." The members of fight club and Project Mayhem, furthermore, once believed in the salvation myth as the narrator did, and, as Hoffer would argue, joined both organizations out of similar feelings of intense disillusionment.

The narrator's search for a father figure ultimately results in the creation of Tyler Durden, but within Durden is the narrator's ability to transcend the need for a father, a fact that results in the existentialist nature of Durden's *weltanschauung*. In the soap-making sequence of the film, as lye melts the skin on the narrator's hand, Durden exclaims:

> Our fathers were our models for God. If our fathers bailed, what does that tell you about God? Listen to me. You have to consider the possibility that God does not like you; he never wanted you. In all probability, he hates you. This is not the worst thing that can happen. We don't *need* him. Fuck damnation, man. Fuck redemption. We are God's unwanted children? So be it!

Durden's existential denial of God, in other words, is the outermost expression of the narrator's desire to deny his own father.

The denial of the father, the denial of God, and the symbolic brotherhood of Project Mayhem relate to the salvation myth of technology because, in a postmodern society, technology has *replaced* the traditional standard of the family. Postmodern technology *is* the new god, the new brotherhood, the new standard of safety and security, and consequently the new myth of society. The new myth, however, is a catastrophic cultural development, the duplicity of which the narrator has been trapped in for most of his adult life. In the film, for example, Durden refers to an airline safety card as "the illusion of safety," while the narrator's job as a recall coordinator forces him to evaluate the monetary value of human lives when products his company manufactures fail to work and result in car crashes. Furthermore, as the narrator learns, no tools or conveniences, however interactive, can truly mimic the real value of human interaction. The narrator's final, subconscious aim is actually to return to the realm of familial interaction where he believes he once failed. Once there, he can abandon the salvation myth forever. Project Mayhem is not only an extension of the narrator's rage, but also a messianic need to save everyone in the world from the salvation myth and restore a sense of community and family.

The narrator's quest, in mythological terms, is a heroic one. Throughout much of history, the advancement of technological knowledge has been a process of pain and sacrifice. The heroes were not necessarily those who invented the technology, but rather those, like the human sacrifices of a long-forgotten civilization, who made the technology possible. The narrator's descent into the darkest self-destructive realms of his psyche is, as Campbell describes similar quests, a heroic journey into a mythological hell to save humanity. The narrator's quest, meanwhile, is novel due to its postmodern context. In *Fight Club*, the true salvation of humanity can only be achieved when the current society's salvation myth is destroyed. To destroy the salvation myth, the history of the culture that produced it must first be eradicated. The protagonists' obsession with "hitting bottom" is the liberating sacrifice, the antithesis of the salvation myth that will make it possible to erase history. Campbell notes that all heroic quests feature some boon that the hero will bring back from the depths to save society. In the postmodern world of *Fight Club*, however, the boon is the cataclysmic collapse of society itself. The narrator's liberating sacrifice occurs when he fully accepts Tyler Durden—both as a part of himself and as the father he always lacked—and is able to overcome that duality with a self-inflicted gunshot to the head. It is at the moment when the narrator pulls the trigger that his reconciliation with his father is complete. In Project Mayhem, the amoral fathers and false gods of postmodern technology are the literal enemies. The sacrifices made by the members of Project Mayhem are sacrifices made for us all. In sum, the protagonists of *Fight Club* are truly anti-Christ figures in that they seek to redeem the world on a temporal scale; there is no salvation in the afterlife of Durden's vision of the universe. The only salvation is to be found here and now, in the world we live in, and the boon Project Mayhem brings is the very seed of society's destruction. As the narrator says early in the film, "Fight club was mine and Tyler's gift to the world."

Works Cited

Avishai, Bernard. "America's Invisible Export": *Civilization*, Aug–Sep 2000, 84–88.

Berger, Peter L., and Thomas Luckmann. *The Social Construction of Reality: A Treatise in the Sociology of Knowledge*. New York: Doubleday, 1966.

Campbell, Joseph. *The Hero with a Thousand Faces*, 2nd ed. Princeton: Princeton University Press, 1968.

Hoffer, Eric. *The True Believer: Thoughts on the Nature of Mass Movements*. New York: HarperCollins, 1951.

Holton, Robert. "Globalization's Cultural Consequences," *Annals of the American Academy of Political and Social Science* 570 (2000): 140–153. *Academic Search Elite*. EBSCOhost. Baron-Forness Lib., Edinboro. September 15, 2000. 30 pars.

Leach, Edmund. *Culture and Communication: The Logic by which Symbols Are Connected*. Cambridge: Cambridge University Press, 1976.

Mander, Jerry. "Eleven Inherent Rules of Corporate Behavior," *Earth Island Journal* 10 (2000): 30–32. *Academic Search Elite*. EBSCO-host. Baron-Forness Lib., Edinboro. September 28, 2000. 33 pars.

————."The Dark Side of Globalization": *Nation*, July 15, 1996: 9–14. *Academic Search Elite*. EBSCOhost. Baron-Forness Lib., Edinboro. September 28, 2000. 25 pars.

Marcus, Steven. "Culture and Anarchy Today," *Southern Review* 29 (1993): 433–453. *Academic Search Elite*. EBSCOhost. Baron-Forness Lib., Edinboro. September 12, 2000. 32 pars.

Merelman, Richard M. "Technological Cultures and Liberal Democracy in the United States," *Science, Technology and Human Values* 25 (2000): 167–195. *Academic Search Elite*. EBSCOhost. Baron-Forness Lib., Edinboro. October 11, 2000. 102 pars.

Pacey, Arnold. *The Culture of Technology*. Cambridge: MIT Press, 1983.

Romney, Jonathan. "Boxing Clever": *New Statesman*. November 15, 1999: 43–44. *Academic Search Elite*. EBSCOhost. Baron-Forness Lib., Edinboro. August 21, 2000. 11 pars.

Rutten, Andrew. "Can Anarchy Save Us from Leviathan?" *Independent Review* 3 (1999): 581–594. *Academic Search Elite*. Baron-Forness Lib., Edinboro. September 15, 2000, 32 pars.

David McNutt is a Ph.D. candidate in the field of theology and the arts at the University of Cambridge, England, where he is studying under the supervision of Prof. Jeremy Begbie. He has previously earned degrees at the University of St. Andrews (M.Litt., in conjunction with its Institute for Theology, Imagination and the Arts), Princeton Theological Seminary (M.Div.), and Pepperdine University (B.A. in religion). He is originally from California, and his interests include film, literature, golf, and preparing with his wife Jennifer for the arrival of their first child.

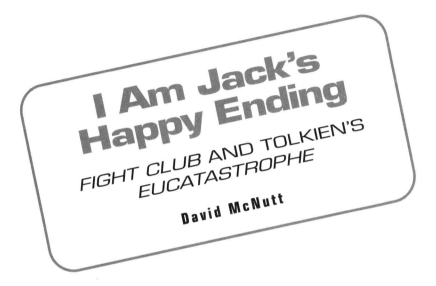

I Am Jack's Happy Ending
FIGHT CLUB AND TOLKIEN'S EUCATASTROPHE
David McNutt

n J.R.R. Tolkien's masterpiece of fantasy literature, The Lord of the Rings, as Frodo and Sam struggle through their harrowing journey, they speak about the nature of stories and their endings. Sam asks,

> "I wonder what sort of a tale we've fallen into?"
>
> "I wonder," said Frodo. "But I don't know. And that's the way of a real tale. Take any one that you're fond of. You may know, or guess, what kind of a tale it is, happy-ending or sad-ending, but the people in it don't know. And you don't want them to."

Those viewing David Fincher's film adaptation of Chuck Palahniuk's novel *Fight Club* may wonder, *What sort of a tale have I fallen into? Will it have a happy ending or a sad ending?* After watching the movie, however, those questions may remain unanswered. At the conclusion of the film, the nameless narrator—shot and bleeding as buildings collapse around him—appears to believe, and leads us as viewers to believe, that he has experienced a happy ending to his story. But is this really the case?

After all, this same narrator, who so willingly embraced Tyler Durden's vision of the world and his notion of salvation through destruction—first through individual conflict in fight clubs, and later through the society-wide damage of Project Mayhem—was soon running from his savior, only to discover that Durden originated within his own mind. So, if the narrator has found a happy ending, is this film advocating the notion that the destruction of civilization is a worthy goal? Is it espousing the idea that the answer to life's difficulties lies in self-destruction? Or is there an alternative message within this story that gives it a "happy" ending?

With those questions in mind, this essay will consider *Fight Club* in light of Tolkien's notion of *eucatastrophe*, the word that he coined to mean "the sudden joyous 'turn'" at the end of stories in the face of overwhelming loss, a miraculous salvation in the midst of great tragedy. At this point, one might normally offer a spoiler warning, but since this entire essay is about the end of stories, both filmed and written, I hope that you'll take one as implied.

Fairy-Stories, Green Knights, and Hobbits: Defining Tolkien's Eucatastrophe

Judged by commentator T.A. Shippey to be "the author of the [twentieth] century," J.R.R. Tolkien is perhaps best known as the creative force behind The Lord of the Rings. Throughout his career—first as the professor of Anglo-Saxon and later of English language and literature at the University of Oxford—Tolkien lectured on literary history and interpretation while producing his own creative work. A devout Roman Catholic, Tolkien was also a member of the Inklings, an informal group of Oxford professors and friends—including C.S. Lewis, Charles Williams, and Owen Barfield—who met on a regular basis to debate a wide range of topics and to read their works-in-progress to each other.

Among Tolkien's academic writing was his seminal essay "On Fairy-Stories"—originally delivered as a lecture at the University of St. Andrews, Scotland, in 1939—in which he discussed his own craft after writing *The Hobbit* and before completing the large-scale project of The Lord of the Rings. As he describes in this essay, fairy-stories are, for Tolkien, not merely stories concerning diminutive creatures called fairies. They are not supernatural tales, or simple stories for children, or falsehoods. Rather, these are stories that draw upon what he calls the world of Faërie. While Tolkien does not offer an explicit definition of Faërie, he does mention that it is "magic of a peculiar mood and power," and he describes the desire at the heart of Faërie as "the realisation, independent of the conceiving mind, of imagined wonder." This world, then, is where the whole breadth and depth of the human imagination comes alive, and fairy-stories are those stories that utilize this capacity.

Drawing upon his or her imaginative skills, Tolkien writes, the story-maker creates "a Secondary World which your mind can enter." While inside that world, what the author conveys is "true," in the sense that "it accords with the laws of that world," and the reader may "therefore believe it, while you are, as it were, inside." Tolkien believed that the art of creating secondary worlds and making myths is an essential part of humanity's existence. This notion was revealed in a poem that he dedicated to his longtime friend and fellow Oxford professor C.S. Lewis. Before Lewis had come to value the ability of myth to convey truth, and before he had written his own classic of children's fantasy, The Chronicles of Narnia, he had told Tolkien that myths were "lies and therefore worthless, even though 'breathed through silver.'" With that in mind, Tolkien dedicated a poem on myth-making, "Mythopoeia," to Lewis. It reads, in part:

> The heart of man is not compound of lies,
> but draws some wisdom from the only Wise,

and still recalls him. Though now long estranged,
man is not wholly lost nor wholly changed.
Dis-graced he may be, yet is not dethroned,
and keeps the rags of lordship once he owned,
his world-dominion by creative act:
not his to worship the great Artefact,
man, sub-creator, the refracted light
through whom is splintered from a single White
to many hues, and endlessly combined
in living shapes that move from mind to mind.
Though all the crannies of the world we filled
with elves and goblins, though we dared to build
gods and their houses out of dark and light,
and sow the seeds of dragons, 'twas our right
(used or misused). The right has not decayed.
We make still by the law in which we're made.

In the tradition of predecessors such as George MacDonald, Tolkien thought that drawing upon our imaginations to make myths and to tell stories—thereby becoming "sub-creators"—was part of humanity's fulfillment of our God-given purpose as he explains in "On Fairy-Stories": "Fantasy remains a human right: we make in our measure and in our derivative mode, because we are made: and not only made, but made in the image and likeness of a Maker." That ability to participate in God's creativity through sub-creation—while clearly distinct from and subordinate to divine creation—is achieved best, in Tolkien's estimation, in the fairy-story, for "in such 'fantasy', as it is called, new form is made; Faërie begins; Man becomes a sub-creator." As Trevor Hart states in "Tolkien, Creation, and Creativity," human artistic creativity is never *creatio ex nihilo*, yet it should be "rooted in a delight in the world for its own sake and desiring nothing more than the world's own good, its enhancement, and the fulfillment of possibilities latent within it."

Importantly, Tolkien located the essential element to a true fairy-story in its ending. Although he believed that drama's true form was tragedy, he found the authentic form of fairy-stories in its opposite.

Because he could not find an existing word to express this idea, Tolkien—ever the sub-creator—decided to invent one: *eucatastrophe*. The word includes the prefix "eu-," meaning "good" (one may think of "eulogy": good words or praise; "euphoria": a good or even great feeling; or "Eucharist": thankfulness for good grace), and the root "strophe," the Greek word for "turn." Eucatastrophe is, quite literally, a good turn of events. But Tolkien meant much more than that.

According to Tolkien, eucatastrophe is an abrupt change in the face of disaster, "a sudden and miraculous grace: never to be counted on to recur." It is a completely unexpected and undeserved rescue in the midst of tragedy, a fortunate ending through unfortunate means. It is that moment when all appears to be lost, but then—incredibly, unbelievably—all is saved and restored. It is, as Ruth Noel describes in *The Mythology of Middle-Earth*, "when imminent evil is unexpectedly averted and great good succeeds." Within this event of "happy calamity," as Ralph C. Wood labels it in *The Gospel According to Tolkien*, there exists an element of providence. John Davenport asserts in "Happy Endings and Religious Hope" that because it is "a surprise, a deliverance that no human effort could have made possible," the eucatastrophic moment "must be experienced not as an achievement of triumphant revenge, but rather as a divine gift."

Significantly, Tolkien notes that the presence of eucatastrophe does not deny the existence of and possibility for *dyscatastrophe*, a real catastrophe. The turn at the end of fairy-stories is preceded by disaster, and there must, Tolkien writes, exist the possibility for a genuine catastrophe—for "sorrow and failure"—in order for "the joy of deliverance" to be authentic. What eucatastrophe does deny, however, is "(in the face of much evidence, if you will) universal final defeat." In this way, fairy-stories provide sincere consolation to the tragic, mournful facets of life. Thus, although formed within humanity's imagination and in a sense not "true," fairy-stories, as Wood explains, "strike deeper truth than other literary forms precisely because of their happy endings—not in spite of them." Tolkien, who perceived much truth in fairy-stories and myth-making, describes the turn at the end of fairy-stories as giving "a catch of the breath, a beat and lifting of the heart, near to (or indeed accompanied by) tears." It is, for him, that eucatastrophic turn in the midst of tragedy that leads to a truly happy ending.

Tolkien identified such a turning in a late fourteenth-century poem that he translated into modern English, "Sir Gawain and the Green Knight." Written by an unknown author, the metrical romance survives in a single manuscript, found in the British Library. The poem, which Tolkien labeled "one of the masterpieces of fourteenth-century art in England, and of English Literature as a whole," presents the story of Sir Gawain, one of the knights of King Arthur's Round Table.

The tale begins at Camelot, where King Arthur's court—including Gawain, the youngest of the knights—is celebrating New Year's Day. Their merriment is disrupted by the intrusion of the enormous Green Knight, mounted on horseback and wielding an axe, who challenges one of King Arthur's knights to step forward and strike him once with his axe on the condition that, should he survive, the Green Knight will return the deed one year and one day later. Just as King Arthur is about to accept the trial, Gawain intercedes, undertakes the challenge, and strikes the intruder, chopping off his head. However, still alive, the Green Knight picks up his own head and, before leaving, reminds Gawain to meet him at the Green Chapel in a year and a day. As Tolkien explains in an essay on the poem, "Gawain is now pledged to a perilous quest and journey the only probable end of which will be his death."

Nearly a year later, with the fateful day approaching, Gawain sets off to find the Green Chapel, eventually stopping at a castle, where he is welcomed by Bertilak, the lord of the castle, and his beautiful wife. Before leaving for a hunt the next day, Bertilak offers a pact to Gawain, which he accepts: the lord will give to Gawain anything that he catches on the hunt, and Gawain will give to the lord whatever he obtains that day. On the first two days, while Bertilak is hunting, his wife attempts to seduce Gawain, who refuses her advances. However, on the third day, he accepts from her a green silk girdle—a kind of belt—which supposedly has the power to protect him from harm. When the lord returns, Gawain fails to give him the girdle, hoping instead to use it in his encounter with the Green Knight.

The following day, Gawain arrives at the Green Chapel to fulfill his promise, and it appears that nothing—not even a magical garment hidden under his armor—will save Gawain from certain death:

> Then the great man in green gladly prepared him,
> gathered up his grim tool there Gawain to smite;
> with all the lust in his limbs aloft he heaved it,
> shaped as mighty a stroke as if he meant to destroy
>   him.
> Had it driving come down as dour as he aimed it,
> under his dint would have died the most doughty
>   man ever.

Just as the axe is about to strike Gawain, the Green Knight pulls the blade back. Again, he does the same thing to Gawain, but on the third blow:

> Lightly his weapon he lifted, and let it down neatly
> with the bent horn of the blade towards the neck
>   that was bare;
> though he hewed with a hammer-swing, he hurt him
>   no more
> than to snick him on one side and sever the skin.

Thus, in a moment of looming catastrophe, Gawain's imminent death is avoided by the Green Knight's completely unexpected mercy. The Green Knight then explains that he is in fact Bertilak, and that Gawain's sojourn at the castle was a tryst meant to examine his character. The third blow, which cut his neck, was meant as punishment for Gawain's acceptance of the green girdle and his failure to disclose it. Such eucatastrophic myth-making led Tolkien to label the poem "a fairy-tale for adults, full of life and colour."

It is, however, in Tolkien's own creative work that one can witness most clearly his concern with eucatastrophe. For the best example of this, look no further than The Lord of the Rings, Tolkien's fantasy epic concerning the history of Middle-earth, the secondary world that he first unveiled in *The Hobbit*. Continuing the story, he tells the adventures of Frodo Baggins, a hobbit from the halcyon land of the Shire, who is commissioned with the imperative duty to destroy the One Ring. Because of its immense power and the evil intentions of Sauron to rule Middle-earth, the Ring must be destroyed by being thrown into the fire in the Cracks of Mount Doom. Accompanying Frodo on his journey is a fellowship representing the races of the free peoples of Middle-earth: Frodo's hobbit friends, Samwise, Meriadoc, and Peregrin; Legolas the elf; Gimli the dwarf; Boromir, son of the steward of Gondor; Aragorn, heir to the throne of Gondor; and a wizard, Gandalf the Grey.

Pursued throughout their task by Ringwraiths, the servants of Sauron, and hounded by Gollum, a former possessor of the Ring, the fellowship endures several disasters, including the fall of Gandalf in his battle with the Balrog, the betrayal and death of Boromir, the separation of Frodo and Sam from the rest of the company, the capture of Merry and Pippin, and Frodo's deterioration under the power of the Ring. However, along the way, there are several brief moments of eucatastrophe. In the estimation of Gunnar Urang, these "lesser 'happy endings' prefiguring the ultimate triumph" include Tom Bombadil's rescue of the Hobbits from the Barrow-wights, the crossing of the River Bruinen, Gandalf's reappearance, the victory at Helm's Deep, and the triumph on the Pelennor Fields. "In every one of these," Urang writes in *Shadows of Heaven*, "despair is abruptly transformed to joy by a sudden and unexpected display of power."

Nearing the conclusion of his mission, Frodo, weak from exhaustion, is carried near the fire of Mount Doom by Sam. But, standing on the precipice and within sight of the completion of his task, Frodo falls to the corruptive powers of the Ring: "'I have come,' he said. 'But I do not choose now to do what I came to do. I will not do this deed. The Ring is mine!'" Tragically, as Wood describes, "Thus does the Quest end not in jubilant victory but disappointing defeat, as Tolkien deflates all his readers' hopes for a conventional heroic ending." However, those who have read the books—or seen

Peter Jackson's recent film adaptations—know that this is not the end of the story. For here, in the moment of defeat, echoes the sound of eucatastrophe. Gollum—who is only alive due to Frodo's mercy and pity for him—suddenly appears, struggles with Frodo, and bites off his finger in order to capture the Ring:

> "Precious, precious, precious!" Gollum cried. "My Precious! O my precious!" And with that, even as his eyes were lifted up to gloat on his prize, he stepped too far, toppled, wavered for a moment on the brink, and then with a shriek he fell. Out of the depths came his last wail *Precious*, and he was gone.

Thus, the Ring is destroyed, but only in a completely unexpected fashion. Moreover, in Tolkien's dénouement to the story, the eucatastrophic moment extends even after the unmaking of the Ring. Surrounded by fire and destruction, Frodo confesses to Sam his resignation to death: "Hopes fail. An end comes. We have only a little time to wait now. We are lost in ruin and downfall, and there is no escape." However, the two companions are suddenly rescued by eagles, who carry them to safety. The completely unanticipated joy encountered in the moment of eucatastrophe is perhaps best demonstrated by Sam, who wakes in Ithilien in the presence of a familiar friend:

> "Gandalf! I thought you were dead! But then I thought I was dead myself. Is everything sad going to come untrue? What's happened to the world?"
>
> "A great Shadow has departed," said Gandalf, and then he laughed, and the sound was like music, or like water in a parched land; and as he listened the thought came to Sam that he had not heard laughter, the pure sound of merriment, for days upon days without count. It fell upon his ears like the echo of all the joys he had ever known. But he himself burst into tears. Then, as a sweet rain will

pass down a wind of spring and the sun will shine out the clearer, his tears ceased, and his laughter welled up, and laughing he sprang from his bed.

Throughout Tolkien's entire corpus, whether in his academic analysis of fairy-stories, his interpretation and translation of ancient literature, or his own creative writing, the theme of eucatastrophe resonates as a central element within his work.

The Ultimate Eucatastrophe

In spite of all his own efforts, Tolkien believed that "the greatest and most complete conceivable eucatastrophe" was to be found in the Christian narrative. "The Gospels contain a fairy-story," he wrote in "On Fairy-Stories," "or a story of a larger kind which embraces all the essence of fairy-stories." Within the Christian account of God's relationship with humanity, Tolkien understood the birth of Jesus Christ to be the eucatastrophe of humanity's history, and he considered Christ's resurrection to be the eucatastrophe in the story of the incarnation. Thus, the story of the joyful triumph of the empty tomb after Jesus' death on the cross is one of "sheer defeat overcome by sheer victory" (Wood). Moreover, in contrast to those myths made by humans, Tolkien stated, "this story has entered History and the primary world; the desire and aspiration of sub-creation has been raised to the fulfilment of Creation." Famously, Tolkien presented this argument to C.S. Lewis—that myth has become fact, that in Colin Duriez's words from *A Field Guide to Narnia*, "the biblical Gospels have all the best qualities of pagan myth, with the unique feature that the events actually happened in documented history"—in a conversation that ultimately led to Lewis's conversion to Christianity.

Several scholars have noted that Tolkien's secondary world of Middle-earth is void of religious language or practice. For example, William Dowie asserts in his essay "The Gospel of Middle-Earth according to J.R.R. Tolkien" that The Lord of the Rings "has no mention of God as such, nothing like worship, and no hint of organized religion; and in this sense it could be readily incorporated into the corpus of modern literature which operates within the experience of a *Deus absconditus*." However, throughout his work there are hints of Tolkien's Christian faith. For example, in *J.R.R. Tolkien: Author of the Century*, Shippey suggests that it is no coincidence that the fellowship sets out from Rivendell on December 25th and completes its task on March 25th, the traditional date of the crucifixion of Jesus. Thus, he writes, the main action of the novel takes place "in the mythic space between Christmas, Christ's birth, and the crucifixion, Christ's death." Other examples—such as the affirmation of the created order in Middle-earth, the sustenance of the elven food *lembas*, the gifts of the princess Galadriel, the temptation to seize the Ring, Gandalf's reemergence, and the triumphant return of Aragorn to the throne of Gondor—could each be expounded upon for their Christian significance. But more important than any one example is Tolkien's belief that the essential eucatastrophic element of fairy-stories was located fundamentally within the story of the Christian faith. Rather than writing an explicit Christian allegory, Tolkien fashioned a story based upon "the ultimate reprieve" of Christ's resurrection (Davenport). In so doing, he points to the true nature of eucatastrophe and thereby brings insight to the story before us.

Fight Club and Eucatastrophe

Through *Fight Club* we enter into a kind of secondary world and encounter a story of constantly shifting expectations and realities. In Fincher's 1999 film, the narrator (Edward Norton) is a young professional who, despite his material comfort, is isolated, unsatisfied, and frustrated with the lack of meaning in his life. Although he finds a degree of solace by attending support groups for individuals suffering from a variety of diseases and addictions—though nothing is apparently wrong with him—this consolation is taken away from him by the presence of Marla Singer (Helena Bonham Carter), another impostor. Soon after, he develops a friendship with a soap salesman, Tyler Durden (Brad Pitt), with whom the narrator begins fight club: an underground fellowship where men gather to express their anger, vent their frustrations, and earn approval by willingly engaging in one-on-one fights with each other. In the original novel, Palahniuk describes the protagonist's frustration with his life and the appeal of Tyler's thinking:

> Tyler explained it all, about not wanting to die without any scars, about being tired of watching only professionals fight, and wanting to know more about himself.
>
> About self-destruction.
>
> At the time, my life just seemed too complete, and maybe we have to break everything to make something better out of ourselves.

In both the novel and the film, Tyler's vision soon overtakes the narrator, as he falls in a downward spiral, moving from an emotionally destitute conformer to an antisocial malcontent in the belief that self-destruction will benefit him.

> Tyler says I'm nowhere near hitting the bottom, yet. And if I don't fall all the way, I can't be saved. Jesus did it with his crucifixion thing. I shouldn't just abandon money and property and knowledge. This isn't just a weekend retreat. I should run from self-improvement, and I should be running toward disaster. I can't just play it safe anymore.
>
> This isn't a seminar.
>
> "If you lose your nerve before you hit the bottom," Tyler says, "you'll never really succeed."
>
> Only after disaster can we be resurrected.
>
> "It's only after you've lost everything," Tyler says, "that you're free to do anything."

This devolving transformation continues, as evidenced by the narrator's mercurial, aloof relationship with Marla and his alteration into a violent instigator. One night at fight club, he takes his aggression out on the handsome Angel Face, saying, "I felt like destroying something beautiful." Moreover, Tyler's vision of a world without social class or financial indebtedness leads to the recruitment of an army through fight club, which is then assigned with the mission of Project Mayhem:

> It's Project Mayhem that's going to save the world. A cultural ice age. A prematurely induced dark age. Project Mayhem will force humanity to go dormant or into remission long enough for the Earth to recover. . . .
>
> Like fight club does with clerks and box boys, Project Mayhem will break up civilization so we can make something better out of the world. . . .
>
> This was the goal of Project Mayhem, Tyler said, the complete and right-away destruction of civilization.

Eventually, however, the narrator becomes frustrated and aghast at the destruction that Project Mayhem is wreaking, and he begins the exhausting, insomnia-filled process of trying to track down and stop Tyler. The elusive leader manages to avoid him until, in a moment of clarity, the narrator realizes that he *is* Tyler, and that he has been doing everything: all that Tyler has done, all that Tyler has ordered to be done. In the movie, a stunned Norton says flatly, "Please return your seat backs to their full, upright, and locked position. . . . We have just lost cabin pressure." Here, we realize that the secondary world into which we have entered is, in truth, within the narrator's mind.

Friendship then turns to combat, and the narrator's conflict moves inward from fight club to his own mind as he attempts to prevent Tyler from taking control of his life and tries to foil Tyler's plans to destroy the general social fabric. In the conclusion to the film, after several rounds of fighting with himself, the narrator realizes that he is the one holding himself captive at gunpoint, not Tyler. Dramatically, the narrator turns the gun on himself, completing his downward spiral to the point of becoming a self-annihilator.

However, here, in the midst of tragedy—both the narrator's own personal struggle and the greater, impending destruction around him—enters the moment of eucatastrophe. For although the narrator shoots himself, he lives, and in the process he rids himself of Tyler's presence and frees himself from Tyler's dominance. That he would live through such a disastrous event is something completely outside his control, yet he does. That he would be merely wounded—like Sir Gawain, only nicked on the neck—is something approaching the miraculous, yet that's what happens.

Calm and serene in the closing sequence, the narrator takes Marla's hand, saying, "Marla, look at me. I'm really okay. Trust me. Everything's going to be fine." Here, at the end, he appears to be able to begin a genuine relationship with Marla, something that he has been incapable of throughout the film, due to his hallucinations and split personality. Thus, by the final frame—through this turn of events wholly beyond his control—the narrator has survived his own destruction and avoided the catastrophic results of his own actions. Even with buildings collapsing around him, it seems that he has indeed experienced a happy ending.

Interestingly, Fincher's interpretation offers quite a different ending to the story than that originally presented by Palahniuk. In the novel, the narrator, looking for a way to rid himself of Tyler and the madness of Project Mayhem, seeks out his own self-destruction, first at fight club:

> Tonight, I go to the Armory Bar and the crowds part zipper style when I walk in. To everybody there, I am Tyler Durden the Great and Powerful. God and father.
> All around me I hear, "Good evening, sir."
> "Welcome to fight club, sir."
> "Thank you for joining us, sir.". . .
> Because I'm Tyler Durden, and you can kiss my ass, I register to fight every guy in the club that night. Fifty fights. One fight at a time. No shoes. No shirts.
> The fights go on as long as they have to.

However, he fights only three men before slumping to the floor. Due to his failed efforts to destroy Tyler and his desire to save Marla, the narrator soon finds himself under Tyler's control again, this time in the final climactic scene atop the Parker-Morris Building, which is rigged to blow up:

> Four minutes.
> Tyler and me at the edge of the roof, the gun in my mouth, I'm wondering how clean this gun is.
> Three minutes.
> Then somebody yells.
> "Wait," and it's Marla coming toward us across the roof.
> Marla's coming toward me, just me because Tyler's gone. Poof. Tyler's my hallucination, not hers. Fast as a magic trick, Tyler's disappeared. And now I'm just one man holding a gun in my mouth.

But even Marla, accompanied by friends from the various support groups, cannot dissuade the narrator from enacting what he believes to be his only option:

> I'm not killing myself, I yell. I'm killing Tyler. . . .
> And I pull the trigger. . . .
> Of course, when I pulled the trigger, I died. . . .
> And Tyler died.
> With the police helicopters thundering toward us, and Marla and all the support group people who couldn't save themselves, with all of them trying to save me, I had to pull the trigger.

At least, he says that he died. Speaking from "heaven," the narrator describes his new home as a place where everything is "white on white," angels "bring you your meals on a tray with a paper cup of meds," and God sits behind "his long walnut desk with his diplomas hanging on the wall behind him." Thus, in Palahniuk's original ending, it appears that the narrator survives his self-destructive behavior, but he finds himself a patient in a mental institution or psychiatric ward.

The eucatastrophic element to the conclusion of this version of the story is quite different from that in Fincher's film. For although he has unexpectedly survived his self-inflicted gunshot, and although the building doesn't blow up as he intended, the narrator is not free from his delusions about Tyler. In the closing chapter, as people—with broken noses or black eyes—occasionally pass by, they whisper to him, "We miss you, Mr. Durden" or "We look forward to getting you back." Moreover, reproached by society and confined by his own mind, the narrator is still not capable of an authentic relationship, with Marla or anyone else.

Palahniuk's novel thus mutes its own potential for eucatastrophe: the death that the narrator miraculously avoids only serves to point to the greater, unconquered struggle within his mind. Fincher's adaptation, by contrast, introduces a stronger eucatastrophic element and contains a clearer turn, in the midst of tragedy, to a happy ending—one that, I believe, falls within Tolkien's understanding of eucatastrophic myth-making.

Three Degrees of Eucatastrophe: The Fincher Oeuvre

Considering some of Fincher's other films in light of their eucatastrophic implications may lead to a better understanding of the ending of *Fight Club*. Within his work, one may perceive various degrees of eucatastrophe, three examples of which I will explore, although one could equally examine his other films, such as *Alien³* (1992) and *Zodiac* (2007). First, in Fincher's thriller *Se7en* (1995), two homicide detectives—the soon-to-retire veteran William Somerset (Morgan Freeman), and the young, brash David Mills (Brad Pitt)—search for a serial killer who is choosing his victims due to their personification of the seven deadly sins. Leading the detectives from one gruesome crime scene to the next, the "John Doe" killer (Kevin Spacey) believes that his crimes are justified by their exposure of humanity's sins, including gluttony, greed, sloth, lust, and pride. As the tension mounts and the detectives' desperation grows, Somerset says to Mills, "You know this isn't going to have a happy ending. It's not possible."

His foresight proves to be true, for Doe is arrested only when he turns himself in at the police precinct. Although captured, the killer seeks to complete his macabre plan by taking the detectives to a final crime scene. In the wilderness, Doe reveals that he has murdered Mills's wife Tracy (Gwyneth Paltrow) and their unborn child—thus demonstrating his own sin of envy. With his partner utterly heart-broken, Somerset explains to Mills that he has a choice: arrest Doe, as his police duties require of him, or kill him, thereby exemplifying the sin of wrath and completing the killer's plan. With tears in his eyes, Mills shoots Doe.

Se7en offers a compelling examination of not only the sinful activity latent within contemporary society, but also the impossibil-ity for humanity to redeem itself. Interestingly, in an alternate end-ing—unshot, but scripted by storyboards—Somerset rather than Mills shoots Doe at the end, thus thwarting the killer's plan, at least in part, and sacrificing his freedom on behalf of his partner. How-ever, in the completed version of the film, there is no redemption, no moment of grace. To use one of Tolkien's terms, there is only dyscatastrophe.

Secondly, the story of *Panic Room* (2002) follows Meg Altman (Jodie Foster), who, shortly after her divorce, moves with her daugh-ter Sarah (Kirsten Stewart) into a New York City apartment that includes a "panic room," a completely secure and self-contained enclosure designed for protection during a home invasion. Naturally, on their first night in their new home, three thieves—Burnham (For-est Whitaker), Junior (Jared Leto), and Raoul (Dwight Yoakam)—break into the apartment, looking for money left behind by the previous occupant.

Although Meg and Sarah manage to lock themselves in the panic room safely, they soon realize that what the burglars are looking for is located inside the room. After a series of failed efforts on the part of the intruders to break into the enclosure, and on the part of the mother and daughter to get help, it appears that the confrontation has reached a stalemate. However, when Meg's ex-husband shows up at the apartment, the thieves threaten his life. In addition, Sarah's worsening diabetic condition forces Meg to leave the room in search of medicine and food. With Junior shot dead by Raoul, the two remaining burglars access the panic room and the money inside, but they then find themselves locked in the room. After Burnham helps Sarah by giving her a shot of insulin, the thieves attempt their escape. In the melee that ensues, Burnham manages to flee with the money, but Raoul struggles with Meg. Just as he prepares to kill her, Burnham returns and shoots Raoul, thus saving the Altman family. Having delayed his escape, Burnham is captured by the police.

Watching *Panic Room*, viewers encounter what I would label a fleeting moment of eucatastrophe. Burnham's sacrificial action on behalf of the Altmans is certainly a dramatic turn of events. However, it is not necessarily unexpected, especially in light of Burnham's previous care for Sarah. Thus, despite its turn in the midst of tragedy, *Panic Room* does not ultimately—again employing Tolkien's wording in "On Fairy-Stories"—give "a catch of the breath, a beat and lifting of the heart."

Thirdly, however, in *The Game* (1997), Fincher presents an example of genuine eucatastrophe. Nicholas Van Orton (Michael Douglas) is a San Francisco investment banker who, despite his tremendous wealth, leads a life of elite isolation, separated from most of the world, including his family. On his forty-eighth birth-day—which is the same age at which his father committed suicide—Van Orton is surprised by his estranged brother Conrad (Sean Penn), who gives him an invitation to Consumer Recreation Services, a mysterious entertainment firm. His curiosity piqued, Van Orton decides to partake in the offer, but his involvement in "the game" soon leads to a series of increasingly bizarre and dangerous events that invade his privileged world and disrupt his public persona. Van Orton soon discovers that the game is in fact a ruse to access his vast sums of money. However, he is too late to prevent the firm's actions, and he passes out, having been drugged by Christine, one of the firm's employees.

He awakes in a coffin, buried alive in Mexico. Unraveled and ragged, both physically and emotionally, Van Orton begins his long journey home. Collecting a gun from his foreclosed mansion along the way, he infiltrates the firm's offices, where he finds everyone who had played their parts to deceive him, including Christine. Trapped on the roof of the building, she tries to convince Van Orton that everything has just been a game—everything, that is, except the gun that he is holding. But he doesn't believe her, and as the doors to the roof swing open, Van Orton shoots Conrad, who is holding a bottle of champagne. Horrified at having killed his own brother, Van Orton walks to the edge of the building and—like his father before him—jumps to his certain death.

Here enters the sudden turn, the eucatastrophic moment: Van Orton falls through the glass ceiling of the banquet hall below, landing uninjured on a gigantic safety mat, thus both avoiding his death and making a dramatic entrance into his own birthday party. After he is helped to his feet, the stunned Van Orton is greeted by Conrad, who is unharmed, and—after he reveals that everything, including the gun, really *has* been a game—the two brothers embrace. The narrative flow of *The Game* is somewhat similar to *Fight Club* in that the protagonist believes that the world presented to him is reality, when in fact things are quite different. Moreover, as in *Fight Club*, through a series of increasingly disastrous events beyond his control, viewers witness the unraveling of an individual, to the point that he is willing to bring about his own tragic downfall. However, in both cases—through a sudden, unforeseen turn—disaster is averted, and the main character is led into freedom from his previous condition, with the possibility for authentic relationships with others.

Conclusion

On the whole, Fincher's work thus far is undoubtedly gritty, often examining the darker side of human nature and society. Moreover, while the plotlines are engaging, specific scenes can be challenging and even difficult to watch. But within these gloomy, even sinister scenarios exists the possibility—if not always the reality—of unexpected, undeserved change. In that sense, the tragic situations into which Fincher's characters fall provide a context that is open to both true catastrophe and—in some instances, through an unanticipated "good turn" of events—genuine eucatastrophe.

There are, to be sure, several differences between the vision offered by Tolkien's notion of eucatastrophe—as exemplified fundamentally in the Christian faith—and that of *Fight Club*, whether in Fincher's or Palahniuk's version. A few brief observations in this regard will suffice. First, the Christian faith affirms that the salvation narrative of God's relationship with humanity occurred in human history, and, most importantly, was uniquely revealed at a particular time and place within that history in the person of Jesus Christ (John 1:14), not within the inner workings of one person's mind. Secondly, despite the pseudo-community created and embraced by the protagonist through his fight club, he is ultimately concerned with his own fate, whereas the Christian faith—while, in one sense, a matter of individual belief—is only genuinely lived out within a community that seeks to build one another up, rather than tear each other down (1 Cor. 12:13). Finally, and perhaps most importantly, in Christian theology the means to salvation is offered only by God through the incarnation, death, and resurrection of Christ (Col. 1:20), whereas in *Fight Club* the narrator provides his own means to redemption: self-destructive behavior and a loaded gun.

At the same time, however, there are some striking similarities between the Christian vision of redemption and the story of *Fight Club*. There is, first, the theme of the possibility for authentic relationships. As the narrator appears—at least at the end of the film—to be capable of a relationship with Marla, likewise the Christian faith calls for honest, forgiving relationships between believers (Eph. 4:32), and it points to the restored relationship that believers experience with God through Christ by the power of the Holy Spirit (Rom. 5:1). A second common theme is the possibility of a new creation and a new order. Tyler attempts to create a new social structure, but his anarchist vision is sought only through violent revolution. Meanwhile, Christian theology promises not only the reality of believers being made new creations in Christ (2 Cor. 5:17), but also the eschatological revelation of "a new heaven and a new earth" (Rev. 21:1). Finally, the third—and, I think, primary—

thematic connection to be found between these stories is the completely unexpected, undeserved "good turn" at the heart of each one. In this regard, the surprising deliverance experienced by the narrator is reminiscent not only of the unforeseen turns throughout Tolkien's work, but even of that great eucatastrophe that forms the basis of the Christian faith.

With all this in mind, *Fight Club* is, in my opinion, a film that reveals the possibility for joy in the midst of sorrow and victory in the midst of defeat. The completely unanticipated liberation that the narrator experiences thereby points to the reality of a truly miraculous grace.

Works Cited

Carpenter, Humphrey. *J.R.R. Tolkien: A Biography*. London: George Allen & Unwin, 1977.

Davenport, John J. "Happy Endings and Religious Hope: The Lord of the Rings as an Epic Fairy Tale," in *The Lord of the Rings and Philosophy: One Book to Rule Them All*, Gregory Bassham and Eric Bronson, eds. Chicago: Open Court, 2003.

Dowie, William. "The Gospel of Middle-Earth according to J.R.R. Tolkien," in *J.R.R. Tolkien, Scholar and Storyteller: Essays in Memoriam*, Mary Salu and Robert T. Farrell, eds. London: Cornell University Press, 1979.

Duriez, Colin. *A Field Guide to Narnia*. Downers Grove, Illinois: InterVarsity Press, 2004.

Hart, Trevor. "Tolkien, Creation, and Creativity," in *Tree of Tales: Tolkien, Literature, and Theology*, Trevor Hart and Ivan Khovacs, eds. Waco, Texas: Baylor University Press, 2007.

Noel, Ruth S. *The Mythology of Middle-Earth*. London: Thames and Hudson, 1977.

Shippey, T.A. *J.R.R. Tolkien: Author of the Century*. London: HarperCollins, 2000.

Tolkien, Christopher. Foreword to *The Monsters and the Critics and Other Essays*, London: HarperCollins, 1997.

Tolkien, J.R.R. *The Lord of the Rings: The Two Towers*. London: HarperCollins, 1999.

———. *The Lord of the Rings: The Return of the King*. London: HarperCollins, 1999.

———. "Mythopoeia," in *Tree and Leaf*. London: Grafton, 1992.

———. "On Fairy-Stories," in *The Monsters and the Critics and Other Essays*, Christopher Tolkien, ed. London: HarperCollins, 1997.

———. "Sir Gawain and the Green Knight," in *The Monsters and the Critics and Other Essays*. London: HarperCollins, 1997.

———, trans. *Sir Gawain and the Green Knight, Pearl, and Sir Orfeo*. London: George Allen & Unwin, 1975.

Urang, Gunnar. *Shadows of Heaven: Religion and Fantasy in the Writing of C.S. Lewis, Charles Williams, and J.R.R. Tolkien*. London: SCM Press, 1971.

Wood, Ralph C. *The Gospel According to Tolkien: Visions of the Kingdom in Middle-Earth*. Louisville: Westminster John Knox Press, 2003.

This three-paragraph submission to Metaphilm is not, per se, an essay, but contains a gem of an interpretive insight that we don't get anywhere else in this collection, so I've included it here as surplus cocktail party banter.

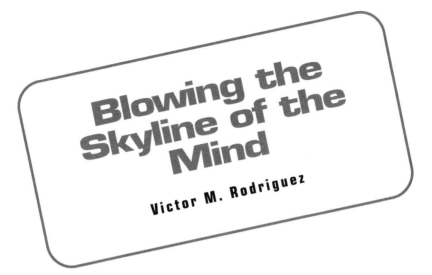

Blowing the Skyline of the Mind

Victor M. Rodriguez

ight Club is about de-conditioning the programs we have been fed, *not about bombing corporations.*

At the end of the movie, when Tyler says something along the lines of "It's too late, you can't do anything, in sixty seconds the bombs are gonna explode and all the system is gonna fall apart"—from that very moment if we count one minute, we get *precisely* to the point when "Jack" shoots himself, literally and metaphorically opening his head. Finally he is freed and able to "jack" (in the sense of *The Matrix*) the memeplex he had been raised into. The actual explosion of the real bombs takes place several minutes later, at the end of the movie.

The soundtrack confirms this on the closing credits when the Pixies sing, "Where is my mind?"

Artist and writer Uri Dowbenko is the author of *Bushwhacked: Inside Stories of a True Conspiracy* and founder of ConspiracyPlanet.com, AlMartinRaw.com, SteamshovelPress.com, and ConspiracyDigest.com. This piece, in its original form, first appeared in *Hoodwinked: Watching Movies With Eyes Wide Open* (Conspiracy Digest, 2004). His Web site is www.UriDowbenko.com.

Fight Club: The Movie Reveals Secrets of Janus Mind Control Programming

Uri Dowbenko

When you see *Fight Club*, you'll have "front row seats for the theater of destruction." Or so promises the movie poster.

Ostensibly a film about underground Ultimate Fighting, *Fight Club* is actually an externalized psychodrama and probably the best illustration of the internal workings of a Multiple Personality Disorder (MPD) victim ever made.

MPD has since been reclassified by the American Psychiatric Association as Dissociative Identity Disorder or DID. The Diagnostic and Statistical Manual, known as the "bible of psychiatrists," characterizes this condition by the following symptoms:

- The presence of two or more distinct personality states;
- At least two of these identities or personality states recurrently take control of the person's behavior;

- Inability to recall important personal information that is too extensive to be explained by ordinary forgetfulness;
- The disturbance is not due to the direct physiological effects of a substance or a general medical condition.

Often MPD or DID is produced when an individual experiences or witnesses an involuntary trauma, such as an airplane crash or a massacre. In other cases, alternate personalities are created deliberately using torture, a hallmark of mind control "methodology."

Since trauma-based mind control programming techniques originated in Nazi Germany—and were then transferred after WWII to the United States during Project Paperclip, an OSS-CIA sponsored resettlement of about 2,000 high-level Nazis in the United States—the technology has advanced rapidly.

"The Germans under the Nazi government began to do serious scientific research into trauma-based mind control," write Fritz Springmeier and Cisco Wheeler in their book *The Illuminati Formula Used to Create an Undetectable Total Mind Controlled Slave*. "Under the auspices of the Kaiser Wilhelm Medical Institute in Berlin, Josef Mengele conducted mind control research on thousands of twins and thousands of other hapless victims."

Mengele, known as "the Angel of Death," was one of the approximately 900 military scientists and medical researchers secretly exfiltrated and brought into the United States. Here, he continued his so-called "research" in torture and then trained others in the black arts of mind control. This work in behavior manipulation was later incorporated into the CIA's Projects Bluebird and Artichoke which, in 1953, became the notorious Project MKULTRA. The CIA claims that these programs were discontinued, but there is no credible evidence that the project's goal, *The Search for the Manchurian Candidate* (the title of the definitive book by John Marks), ever ceased.

Fight Club is the story of two alters, separate split personalities the narrator (Edward Norton) and his Big Bad Alter ego Tyler Durden (Brad Pitt), who forces a gun into the narrator's mouth in the beginning of the film. The movie then is an extended flashback until the end, as the narrator, through deadpan voiceover, describes his life in a nightmarish first person rant.

The super-alienated narrator works as a zombified analyst for a big car company. He suffers from insomnia, and a doctor, in a spoof of new age medicine, tells him to chew some valerian and get some rest. His bean-counter actuarial job is to figure out how many customer deaths it takes to warrant a product recall, and he spends the rest of his time compulsively ordering home furnishings for his apartment.

Driven by his consumer cult addiction, he starts attending support group meetings to counteract his anomie. "I became addicted to groups," he says, visiting a different twelve-step group every night. There he meets a fellow traveler like himself, the chain-smoking spiky-haired Marla, a tourist who goes to support groups for "diseases" she doesn't have.

Unexpectedly the narrator then meets his alter personality Tyler Durden. Tyler, who wears retro '70s clothes and has a spiked haircut, sneers at the narrator and his unfulfilling meaningless lifestyle, commenting, "You have a kind of sick desperation in your laugh."

When his apartment is blown up, the narrator moves into Tyler's place, a dilapidated war-zone mansion with broken ceilings and a flooded basement that looks like a crack house, saying, "I didn't know if he owned it or if he was squatting." There, Tyler makes liposuction-based soap that he sells to tony boutiques, or as the narrator puts it, "We were selling the rich women their fat asses back to them."

Meanwhile, at night, the boys have organized an underground bare-knuckle boxing club with other disaffected youth. The narrator says, "Every evening I died and every evening I was born again." It's S&M chic with homoerotic undertones. Black and Blue Psycho-Boys beat each other till they drop. "'In Tyler We Trust' was their motto," says the narrator.

Tyler has become a mind control cult leader with "franchises" in every major city. He shaves his recruits' heads and calls them "space monkeys," and his skinhead followers prepare for Project Mayhem, a plan to blow up the infrastructure of American society.

The movie asks, what's the difference between performance art and sabotage? The late new wave composer Karlheinz Stockhausen actually called the destruction of the World Trade Center on 9-11 "the greatest work of art of the 21st Century."

According to recovered survivors of mind control, *Fight Club* is the story of someone who discovers he has Janus–End Time Programming. Janus and End Time Programming refer to hypnotic induction codes in mind control slaves that are used to "activate" so-called "sleepers" like the Ed Norton character, programmed mind control victims who are triggered to perform certain activities of chaos, disruption, and murder, as illustrated in the film by Project Mayhem.

In other words, the narrator's life, like that of many real-life serial killers and bombers, is taken over by his "tasking" to create mayhem in American Life.

"Rule Number One," says the Brad Pitt character in the movie. "Nobody talks about fight club." The subtext is quite simple. It is taboo in America to talk about mind control as a causative agent of "random violence." Remember—the Columbine High School massacre, the DC Sniper murders, and the Virginia Tech massacre have never been framed in the context of mind control. Even Michael Moore's allegedly progressive anti-gun documentary *Bowling for Columbine* ignored this issue.

The Tyler Durden/Brad Pitt role itself is the raging alter, a split-off personality programmed to create chaos out of order. His character is raging at the mind control atrocities he has experienced as well as the perpetrators who created his internal mind controlled system of alters. In fact, Tyler Durden himself tells the narrator, "Hey, you created me. I didn't create some loser alter ego to make myself feel better. Take some responsibility."

"Ed Norton's insomnia represents his 'unknown' activities," says Annie McKenna, whose autobiographical *Paperclip Dolls* is a first-hand account of mind control abuse and her subsequent recovery.*

---

*See www.conspiracyplanet.com/review.cfm?rtype=24.

In an interview, McKenna said she was stunned by the accurate portrayal of mind control programming in the movie.

"I think the most important message for me was that the rage alter [represented by Brad Pitt] taking over was not going to happen to me. . . . I found it was a very intense message and ending." She continues, "That part where the Ed Norton character realized his insomnia was actually because he was being Tyler, instead of sleeping, was so real. I wonder if the author knew how real that was."

(It is unknown if the author of *Fight Club* Chuck Palahniuk is himself a mind control survivor.)

"The movie was about Brad Pitt (the rage alter) slowly taking over the formerly dominant personality," says McKenna. "And look what it related to—organized armies and destruction. It was very intense programming that was planned for the year 2000."

It should be noted that the destruction of the World Trade Center, better known by its shorthand "9-11," occurred on September 11, 2001—a mere year after the New Millennium.

McKenna says she doesn't know the origin of this mind control programming. "I just know I got two messages, and I don't know if one is a cover for the other." She continues, "One is self-destruction, but usually it is accompanied by taking others with us. This you have been seeing in the news all over the country, but I'm sure Mainstream America would have a hard time seeing that as programmed mind control victims. The second message is a job in the New World Order."

By "New World Order," she means the integration of various nations and governments into a Global Dictatorship by the Ruling Class or Super Elite.

"This was the meaning of Project Monarch," says McKenna, referring to the notorious mind control project of the U.S. government. "It was birth to death programming—'death' being the end of 'me,' whoever 'me' was when the programming took over and new alters took over the conscious self, responding to automatic pilot programming.

"The end is so unsettling because the Norton character tries to commit suicide, part of the year 2000 programming, but he survives.

Unfortunately his alter completed the mission he had [blowing up the buildings]. So it was a totally ironic ending," McKenna concludes in her analysis.

Meanwhile Ed Norton's character, the narrator, undergoes a PF or Programming Failure and realizes what is happening to him. This occurs "when the programming doesn't take, or a person goes psychotic, so you have to put them down," says a former mind control programmer who goes by the pseudonym Svali.

Fight Club director David Fincher (*Alien*[3], *Se7en,* and *The Game*) is obviously gearing up to do the next U.S. Army recruiting commercials. Who else could capture the S&M brutality and the homoerotic fantasies of military life? The fascist rituals of shaving hair creating Killer Baldheads and the institutional brutality of the Fight Club's Cult of Death have never been so lovingly filmed as in this movie.

Fight Club is a movie about mind control. Think *Raising Cain* on bad acid. Or an ironic and too-hip-for-you update of *A Clockwork Orange* with a brave new mélange of Psychopathic Violence Chic.

The film is also a ceremonial psychodrama, intent on the engineering of the mind, as seemingly normal individuals are transformed into mind controlled robotic assassins or bombers.

Will the film trigger other "sleepers" to fulfill their "tasking"? Only time will tell. But the final explosion, which blows up the Century City skyline of L.A., is like a cinematic bitch-slap that is also an ironic prophecy of the horrendous events of 9-11.

Even though the film was released prior to 9-11, there is an uncanny cinematic foreshadowing of real-life events. Even the first lines of the movie's dialogue are spooky enough to give pause. Tyler points a gun into the narrator's mouth while he speaks in a voiceover, saying, "People are always asking me if I know Tyler Durden." Then Tyler Durden says, "Three minutes. This is it—Ground Zero."

Ground Zero, of course, is also used to reference the location of the former World Trade Center in New York City.

Then the narrator says, "For a second I totally forgot about Tyler's whole controlled demolition thing and I wonder how clean that gun is."

"Controlled demolition," of course, is one of the current explanations for the strange pancake-like fall of the Twin Towers on 9-11.

After all, *Fight Club* lets you peek into a secret and even occult world of covert conspiracy. It ain't pretty, but the next time you hear about a "lone nut assassin" or a "lone nut bomber"—Think Mind Control. . . .

E.J. Park was the cofounder of Metaphilm (www.metaphilm.com) and now lives in Chicago.

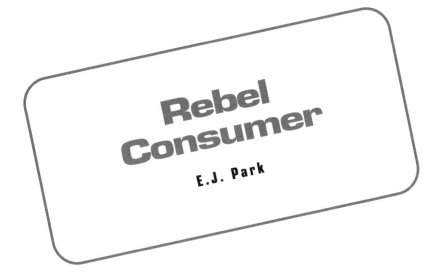

Rebel Consumer

E.J. Park

After watching *Fight Club*, I resolved to change, to be different, to rebel.

I would no longer frequent Starbucks, no longer wear Old Navy, no longer listen to 'N Sync. I was determined to resist consumer culture with a vengeance.

So I went shopping. If you're going to be Tyler Durden, you have to have the right look, the right style, the right kick-ass vibe. At Urban Outfitters, you can buy a wardrobe of dissent for less than six hundred dollars. All the products there have that *fuck you* attitude, which is to say they all appear to be worn-out and retro-fied. Shopping at Urban Outfitters gives you instant "rebel" credibility. Tyler may mock Gap, but he's not going to mock a store that sells Atari T-shirts for twenty-eight bucks. Hell, just visit the nearest Urban Outfitters, and you'll see Tyler Durdens and Marla Singers everywhere. I ended up spending $565 for a jacket, a pair of leather pants, and three Ben Sherman button-down shirts. Afterward, I got myself a tattoo that says FUCK CONSUMERISM. I felt so liberated, so free from the mass conformity of our commercialized culture. I felt like one of those rebels in the "defy convention" Reebok ads, transgressing the "norms" of our civilized society. Inspired, I got online

117

and immediately ordered a pair of Pump Fury Reeboks for $109.99, and then I downloaded the "defy convention" screensaver for inspiration. Before I disconnected, I went on eBay and made a bid for a bar of pink *Fight Club* soap. I couldn't think of a better way to remind myself of the mindless consumerism of our age than to buy some pink *Fight Club* soap. I thank Tyler, and *Fight Club*, that I'm no longer a slave to commercial products.

Top Five Rebel Commercials

1. *Fight Club*. (see above)
2. *Disturbing Behavior*. There are two types of people: programmed teens who dress like J. Crew dweebs and free-spirited rebels who sport leather jackets and barbed-wire tattoos. If you want to be a cool individual, shop where Katie Holmes shops.
3. *Grease*. In the end, leather wins! And it has never looked so delicious!
4. *Rebel Without a Cause*. What is a rebellious, restless, misunderstood, middle-class youth to do in the monotone world of suburbia? Wear leather, of course!
5. *The Matrix*. It is our mission to free human civilization from its comatose state. What should we wear? Leather, leather, and more leather! (Oh, and sunglasses.)

Shopping Tips

If you are really serious about rebelling against consumerism, shop at the following stores:

- Urban Outfitters
- Reebok
- Apple

Kirsten Stirling is assistant professor of English at the University of Lausanne in Switzerland. She holds a Ph.D. in Scottish literature from the University of Glasgow. Her current area of research is a word-and-image approach to seventeenth-century religious poetry, particularly the "Holy Sonnets" of John Donne. The following is a revision of a piece that first appeared as "'Dr. Jekyll and Mr. Jackass': *Fight Club* as a refraction of Hogg's *Justified Sinner* and Stevenson's *Jekyll and Hyde*" in *Refracting the Canon in Contemporary British Literature and Film,* edited by Susanna Onega and Christian Gutleben (Amsterdam and New York: Rodopi, 2004). If you don't already know and love the literature of James Hogg, you owe it to yourself to read this piece.

Dr. Jekyll and Mr. Jackass

FIGHT CLUB'S ECHOES OF THE NINETEENTH-CENTURY DOPPELGÄNGER

Kirsten Stirling

Toward the end of David Fincher's film *Fight Club* (1999), the main character tries to apologize to his girlfriend Marla for his recent behavior—"I know I've been acting very, very strange and that it's been like there's two sides of me." She snorts, "Two sides? You're Dr. Jekyll and Mr. Jackass!" Robert Louis Stevenson's *The Strange Case of Dr. Jekyll and Mr. Hyde* (1886) is one of those works of literature whose name has passed into the language and the popular imagination and taken on a life of its own, so it is impossible to claim that this is an explicit reference to Stevenson's novella, and the phrase does not appear in Chuck Palahniuk's novel *Fight Club* (1996), on which the film is based.

Since *Fight Club* is a portrait of a split personality, there are obvious connections to be made between it and *Jekyll and Hyde*. However, *Fight Club's* concern with the role of society in determining the nature of the individual moves it beyond the relatively closed world of Stevenson's novella and suggests comparison with *Jekyll and Hyde's* immediate ancestor, James Hogg's *The Private Memoirs and Confessions of a Justified Sinner* (1824). Although the eighteenth-century Calvinist repression of *Justified Sinner* and the twentieth-century urban nihilism of *Fight Club* are light-years apart, both texts are remarkably close in their representation of the effects on the individual of a society's political and religious ethos, in their study of the perversion of political or religious discourses, and in their exploration of the nature of addiction. I am not suggesting that *Fight Club* is a deliberate attempt to rewrite either of these nineteenth-century novels; it is more a brand of twentieth-century gothic that strongly recalls aspects of both. And in its highly modern reworking of the theme of the doppelgänger, it suggests new ways of reading its nineteenth-century predecessors. My analysis will concentrate more on Fincher's film than on Palahniuk's novel, because although in many ways the film stays very close to the novel, there are certain subtle script changes (the screenplay was written by Jim Uhls) and visual details that tighten the narrative and make the film more referential, and also more ambiguous, than the book.

Like *Jekyll and Hyde*, *Fight Club* exploits the nightmare quality of the nocturnal city. The key passages of horror in *Jekyll and Hyde*—the "Juggernaut" incident where Hyde is witnessed knocking over and trampling the body of a small girl, and the murder of Sir Danvers Carew—take place in empty but well-lit streets in the small hours of the morning: "street after street, all lighted up as if for a procession, and all as empty as a church"; "the early part of the night was cloudless, and the lane . . . was brilliantly lit by the full moon." In both passages the scene is set for a clear eyewitness account of events. The shell of the city functions as the backdrop for events, but its citizens have been removed. In the twentieth-century urban gothic of *Fight Club*, the key scenes take place in empty car parks and basements, the deserted infrastructure of the city. The lighting effects, the contrast of darkness and light, are important in *Fight Club*, as in *Jekyll and Hyde*. The penultimate scene of the film *Fight Club* takes place in a brightly lit but deserted underground car park, where the unnamed narrator and Tyler Durden have their final physical fight. There is no one to witness them, yet on the closed-circuit security camera we see what is *actually* happening: the narrator throwing punches at himself, then pushing himself down a potentially lethal flight of stairs. The unattended security camera gives us an external perspective through the medium of film. The emphasis on the nocturnal city in *Jekyll and Hyde* is equally cinematic, and indeed could be said to foreshadow the invention of the cinema:

> . . . as he lay and tossed in the gross darkness of the night and the curtained room, Mr. Enfield's tale went by before his mind in a scroll of lighted pictures. He would be aware of the great field of lamps of a nocturnal city; then of the figure of a man walking swiftly; then of a child running from the doctor's; and then these met, and that human Juggernaut trod the child down and passed on regardless of her screams.

The "scroll of lighted pictures" irresistibly brings to mind the cinema, but so does Stevenson's cinematic technique here of cutting between characters and scenes to create suspense. In both books we also see the house becoming a metaphor for the split and chaotic self. As Nabokov points out, in *Jekyll and Hyde*, the two doors of Jekyll's house, one opening onto a "large, low-roofed, comfortable hall" and the other "blistered and distained" leading to the old dissecting room and used by Mr. Hyde, are an indication of the contradictions within the man. In *Fight Club*, the house in Paper Street, filling up with water in rainy weather, waiting to be torn down, becomes a similar metaphor for the mental state of its inhabitant(s).

The stage is set for the appearance of the double. But the big question is: Where does the double come from? In *The Divided Self*, Masao Miyoshi outlines the basic distinction regarding the source of the second or other self: "in the case of duplication, the second self or double appears, as it were, from outside the first self; whereas in the case of division, as in the Jekyll–Hyde personality, it splits off from within." *Jekyll and Hyde*, as Miyoshi points out, is the classic example of division, of the internal double who comes from within the first self and is a projection of an aspect of the first self. But the doppelgänger may also seem to come from without, and even if this second, external self functions in a similar way, that is, to complete or complement the personality of the first self, the encounter of the doubles is necessarily different.* In *Jekyll and Hyde* the key moment of confrontation between the doubles is in the mirror, when Jekyll recounts his moment of recognition of his Hyde-self with the words "This, too, was myself." In Hogg's *Justified Sinner*, the encounter with the double is not obviously one of self-division, as Robert Wringhim clearly witnesses the approach of his double:

> I beheld a young man of mysterious appearance coming towards me. . . . As we approached each other, our eyes met and I can never describe the strange sensations that thrilled through my whole frame at that impressive moment. . . . That strange youth and I approached each other in silence, and slowly, with our eyes fixed on each other's eyes. We approached till not more than a yard intervened between us, and then stood still and gazed, measuring each other from head to foot. What was my astonishment on perceiving that he was the same being as myself!

The slow approach of the doppelgänger, together with the emphasis on looking, seems to establish this relationship as one of duplication rather than division, yet this impression is never confirmed. The tension in Hogg's *Justified Sinner* depends upon this doubt surrounding

---

*The term *doppelgänger* was coined by Jean Paul Richter in his novel *Siebenkäs* (1796). The classic German example of the theme is E.T.A. Hoffman's *Die Elixiere des Teufels* (1816), in English, *The Devil's Elixirs*.

this question of the source of the double. Does the equivocal and elusive figure of Gil-Martin come from elsewhere—in which case he may be the devil himself—or is he a projection of an aspect of Wringhim's personality, as Hyde is a projection of an aspect of Jekyll? The novel remains strung between the internal and the external double, the psychological and the supernatural.

Palahniuk's novel *Fight Club* offers no supernatural explanation for events. Tyler Durden is not the devil. Neither is Mr. Hyde. In *Jekyll and Hyde*, written sixty years after Hogg's *Justified Sinner*, science, rather than the supernatural, accounts for the appearance of Hyde. Yet the language used to describe Hyde—"hellish"; "damnable"—is supernatural. The supernatural is evoked metaphorically, as if it is easier to describe Hyde, who "alone, in the ranks of mankind, was pure evil," in the terms of Christian binary oppositions, than to acknowledge him as part of the self. While Hyde may be described in Satanic terms—"if ever I read Satan's signature upon a face, it is on that of [Jekyll's] new friend"—there is no place for such supernatural or religious terminology in Palahniuk's or Fincher's urban wasteland. *Fight Club*'s doubling seems firmly psychological, and resides in the revelation that the cool and dangerous Tyler is in fact the alter ego of the unnamed first-person narrator. The process of revelation takes us from the assumption that Tyler is an external double who comes from elsewhere, and leads us to the realization that "Tyler is a projection. He's a disassociative personality disorder. A psychogenic fugue state. Tyler Durden is my hallucination." This is not the language of the devil. And yet, Fincher's film emphasizes the demonic aspects of Tyler Durden. When we see Tyler (Brad Pitt) lurking behind the narrator's left shoulder, in shadow, down a flight of stairs, or whispering words into his ear, or even just grinning his dangerous grin, he becomes closer to a type of updated, leather-jacketed folk devil, a modern version of Hogg's Gil-Martin.

Tyler could not—indeed *should* not—be described in the explicitly demonic terms used in Hogg's *Justified Sinner*, because the discourse that is satirized and undermined in *Fight Club* is not that of religion. Under attack here are firstly the materialist values of modern

American capitalist society, and then secondly Tyler's anti-capitalist discourse. The fight club of the title is the narrator's (and Tyler's) reaction to his anodyne life, his lovingly furnished apartment, and his boring (and morally questionable) job. In bare-fist fighting he discovers a visceral pleasure that relieves him from the pressure to conform to society's expectations. The popularity of fight club suggests that there is a general malaise among young men, and that underground violence offers an alternative way of life that can eventually challenge and threaten the capitalist structures of society. Fight club is only the beginning of Tyler's plan, because after starting a business selling soap made from liposuctioned fat stolen from a nearby clinic, he moves on to form an army with the bands of disaffected young men he has recruited to his underground clubs. The task of this army, known as "Project Mayhem," is to vandalize and destroy various targets of civilized society: blowing out the windows of an office tower to make a (demonic) face, vandalizing phone booths, urinating in food in restaurant kitchens. The schoolboy humor and the sheer attraction of anarchy keep the reader or viewer in a vicarious thrill—until it goes too far. Because of course it goes too far. Does this make Tyler the devil? No. But he is the only possible alternative to the devil in a society without religion. The strict Calvinist upbringing of Robert Wringhim in Hogg's *Justified Sinner*—and the society in which he lives, riven with religious feuds and sectarian rivalry—is the perfect setting for the appearance of a devil who speaks the language of religion. In the society of *Fight Club* Tyler, with his anti-capitalist rhetoric, represents the epitome of what the narrator wants to be: "I look like you want to look, I fuck like you want to fuck . . ." etc. He offers a way to "hit bottom." The cool, leather-jacketed figure of Tyler is the image of everything that is at once desired and dangerous in the narrator's world.

Robert Wringhim is flattered and attracted by the attentions of Gil-Martin—"he had such a way with him, and paid such a deference to all my opinions, that I was quite captivated"—and the introduction of the narrator to Tyler in *Fight Club* works in a very similar way. One significant difference between the film and the book is the way in which the two main characters meet. In the book they meet on a beach, where Tyler is at work building something from drift-wood on the sand:

> What Tyler had created was the shadow of a giant hand. Only now the fingers were Nosferatu-long and the thumb was too short, but he said how at exactly four-thirty the hand was perfect. The giant shadow hand was perfect for one minute, and for one perfect minute Tyler had sat in the palm of a perfection he'd created himself.

In the film they meet on an airplane, and Tyler flatters the narrator's intelligence—though admittedly in a rather ironic way. "You're very clever. . . . How's that working out for you then, being clever?" The film version is much closer to the meeting of Robert Wringhim with Gil-Martin in *Justified Sinner*, when Gil-Martin seduces Robert at first by flattering him:

> Your state is a state to be envied indeed; but I have been advised of it, and am come to be a humble disciple of yours; to be initiated into the true way of salvation by conversing with you, and perhaps by being assisted by your prayers.

Robert's "spiritual pride [is] greatly elevated by this address," and he is won over by the stranger's words. In the film version of *Fight Club*, Tyler's flattery of the narrator functions similarly as introduction and as temptation. Like Gil-Martin, Tyler flatters the narrator by offering him a new and attractive way to view himself, and the narrator succumbs. The book version offers a different temptation: the image of Tyler as temporary perfection. But the temptation to be one with this perfection comes from within the narrator, whereas the temptation by flattery implies an external agency looking for a way in.

The film of *Fight Club* thus plays with the notion of distance, of the difference between inside and outside, internal and external temptation, in a very similar way to that of *Justified Sinner*, and as a film, it is able very subtly to reproduce the effects that Hogg achieves through playing with narrative point of view. The duality of *Justified Sinner* is emphasized by Hogg's narrative technique, whereby the first-person "Confessions of a Sinner" are framed by the editor's narrative, which proves to be of equally dubious reliability. Stevenson too mixes narrative points of view in *Jekyll and Hyde*: The main third-person narrative, seen through the eyes of the lawyer Mr. Utterson, is supplemented by Dr. Lanyon's first-person narrative and Dr. Jekyll's own "Full Statement of the Case." The multiplication of perspectives, external and internal, contributes to the impression of a fragmented self. Palahniuk's first-person narrative achieves the effect of fragmentation through a variety of other devices—clipped sentences, flashbacks, and a mixture of direct speech and thought— but it is difficult for an entirely first-person narrative to achieve the contrast between inside and outside that allows the reader a double perspective on the main character and the events he witnesses. *Fight Club* the film reproduces Palahniuk's first-person narrative by means of the voiceover, but the fact that we are watching the narrator as well as listening to him allows Fincher to exploit the notion of distance between the external and the internal. And a series of subliminal cuts showing the image of Tyler Durden before the narrator has been introduced to him again allow the sharp-eyed viewer a privileged perspective on events. Of course the viewer never achieves a totally external perspective: the trick ending of the film, when the main character realizes that he has in fact been Tyler Durden all along, should come as a surprise. But nonetheless we are granted a certain distance, and the words spoken by the narrator are often undermined or given ironic impact by the images on screen.

Fight Club is also closer to *Justified Sinner* than to *Jekyll and Hyde* in that the privileged first-person access to the narrator's thoughts does *not* give us privileged knowledge as to what is going on. On the contrary, in entering the narrator's head, in each case, we enter a web of confusion. The "labyrinths of lamp-lighted city" of *Jekyll and Hyde* become internalized, and the first-person narration restricts our vision. It is easy to forget that *Jekyll and Hyde*, like *Fight Club*, is structured around the principle of the twist, even though *Jekyll and Hyde's* iconic status means that it is virtually impossible to read the book for the first time without being aware that Jekyll is Hyde. The process of revelation in *Jekyll and Hyde* moves from third-person to first-person narrative. The third-person narrative focusing on Mr. Utterson, which comprises around two-thirds of the novella, merely sets up the mystery, while it is in the first-person narratives of Dr. Lanyon and Dr. Jekyll himself that the twist is first revealed and then elucidated. Although *Jekyll and Hyde* purports to deal with "the thorough and primitive duality of man," the self never disintegrates, so that Jekyll is able to give a convincing and lucid account of his experiments and his liberation of Hyde, only hours before his final transformation and death. The first-person narrative in *Jekyll and Hyde* guarantees us the truth, whereas in *Fight Club* and *Justified Sinner* the first-person narrative complicates the story.

In *Justified Sinner* the object of satire is Calvinist doctrine. Gil-Martin may be the devil himself, persuading Robert into deeper sin by means of rhetorical sophistry, or he may be a symptom of Robert's disturbed mind, an alter ego onto whom he can project responsibility for his actions. Either way, it is by interpreting to the letter the Calvinist doctrines of predestination and antinomianism that Robert justifies to himself his many sins, including his multiple murders. In another, more obvious rewriting of Hogg's novel, Emma Tennant's *The Bad Sister* (1978), the object of satire is no longer Calvinism, but what Tennant judges to be its modern equivalent in generating extreme behavior—"a jumble of Marxism and Tantrism and anything else thrown in." In Tennant's rewriting, the female Gil-Martin figure is able to persuade the main character Jane to murder her father because he is a symbol of paternalism and the "incarnation of capitalism." While Tennant's novel has been described as feminist, as has her rewriting of *Jekyll and Hyde*—*Two Women of London* (1989), subtitled *The Strange Case of Ms. Jekyll and Mrs. Hyde*—both these books function in a similar way to *Fight Club*, satirizing both capitalism and anti-capitalism, both patriarchy and feminism. But like *Justified Sinner*, the ultimate object of the satire in each case is extremism and actions brought about by excessive interpretation. Hogg makes it clear that his satire is on extremism and not Calvinism per se. The minister Blanchard tells Robert:

> Religion is a sublime and glorious thing, the bond of society on earth, and the connector of humanity with the Divine nature; but there is nothing so dangerous to man as the wresting of any of its principles, or forcing them beyond their true bounds: this is of all others the readiest way to destruction.

This seals Blanchard's fate as Robert and Gil-Martin's first victim. In *Fight Club* it is anti-capitalist and anti-materialist principles and rhetoric that are taken to extremes and forced beyond their true bounds. At first the narrator's escape from the traps of consumer society seems positive. The alternative society he (or Tyler) creates is, to begin with, based on principles of self-discovery, something that can only be done, according to Tyler, by trying to "hit bottom." So far, so good, although this process of self-discovery involves a great deal of blood and violence. The rich, creamy bars of soap, made by Tyler from fat liposuctioned from rich women in private clinics (which they sell back "to the very people who paid to have it sucked out. At twenty bucks a bar, these are the only folks who can afford it") is a wonderful metaphor for capitalist society. But at some point, Tyler's plan goes too far. The turning point seems to be when Big Bob dies, shot by the police who believed that he was carrying a weapon. But although the death of a friend works as a symbolic turning point, things have already gone wrong, because the narrator has lost control of his alter ego's plans, and has begun to fear what he might be capable of. And what started as a process of self-discovery begins to move toward a denial of individualism, as Tyler teaches his army of nihilistic young men to chant: "You are not a beautiful and unique snowflake. . . . Our culture has made us all the same. . . . Individually, we are nothing."

It is the changing relationship between the narrator and Tyler in *Fight Club* that really recalls *Justified Sinner* rather than *Jekyll and*

Hyde. Robert's relationship with Gil-Martin begins with attraction, turns very quickly to something more like addiction, and ends with loathing and a chase that culminates in his suicide. The narrator of *Fight Club*'s relationship with Tyler follows a very similar trajectory. Robert describes his parting from Gil-Martin as "a great relief; and yet, before the morrow, [he] wearied and was impatient to see him again." In *Fight Club* too the ambiguous relationship between the narrator and Tyler has this addictive quality to it, and a homoerotic element that is much more pronounced in the film than in the book. Marla and Tyler's relationship makes the narrator jealous of *Marla*, and when Tyler seems to be transferring his confidence and affections to a beautiful young man, the narrator takes the opportunity to smash that man's face the next time they meet in fight club. The homoerotic aspects of Hogg's *Justified Sinner* have been discussed by Eve Kosofsky Sedgwick (1985); the film version of *Fight Club* is able to make this aspect of the relationship with the double much more visible. But the attraction eventually turns to loathing and to some kind of realization of the truth of the situation:

> Either I had a second self, who transacted business in my likeness, or else my body was at times possessed by a spirit over which it had no control, and of whose actions my own soul was wholly unconscious. . . . The worst thing of all was, what hitherto I had never felt, and, as yet, durst not confess to myself, that the presence of my illustrious and devoted friend was becoming irksome to me. When I was by myself, I breathed freer, and my step was lighter; but when he approached, a pang went to my heart, and, in his company, I moved and acted as if under a load that I could hardly endure. What a state to be in! And yet to shake him off was impossible— we were incorporated together—identified with one another, as it were, and the power was not in me to separate myself from him.

In *Fight Club* this is articulated much more forcefully by Tyler himself:

> We're not two separate men. Long story short, when you're awake, you have the control, and you can call yourself anything you want, but the second you fall asleep, I take over, and you become Tyler Durden. . . . I wouldn't be here in the first place if you didn't want me. I'll still live my life while you're asleep, but if you fuck with me, if you chain yourself to the bed at night or take big doses of sleeping pills, then we'll be enemies. And I'll get you for it.

Once the attraction has given way to repulsion and a certain degree of realization, the narrators of both *Justified Sinner* and *Fight Club* seem locked into a course that can only end in suicide. Unlike Hyde, who "fears [Jekyll's] power to cut him off by suicide," both Gil-Martin and Tyler Durden move toward this as their ultimate goal. If Gil-Martin is the devil, his logic is presumably that Robert's suicide will once and for all put his soul beyond the possibility of salvation. In the last section of the confessions of the sinner, Robert recounts his flight from his "dreaded and devoted friend," which ends, however, in a suicide pact. This is Gil-Martin's idea, but Robert takes "some miserable comfort in the idea that my tormentor shall fall with me." Just as, in *Fight Club*, suicide is Tyler's idea: "The last thing we have to do is your martyrdom thing. Your big death thing," and yet the narrator, with a gun in his mouth, yells, "I'm not killing myself. . . . I'm killing Tyler!"

The great difference between the two novels, however, is how the last-act suicide scenario ends. Robert Wringhim does kill himself, in supernatural circumstances, by hanging himself with a piece of rope too thin to have borne the weight of a man. The narrator of *Fight Club* puts the gun in his mouth, pulls the trigger, and yet somehow does not die. Whether or not he has killed Tyler, however, is unclear. In the book he ends up in what seems to be a mental hospital, though he describes it as an Old Testament–style heaven. Occasionally, however, he meets nurses or hospital cleaners with black eyes or broken noses who whisper: "We miss you, Mr. Durden. . . . Everything's going according to the plan. . . . We look forward to getting you back." The plan that Tyler has set in motion is continuing— like the devil, he is not so easy to escape from. The film, on the other hand, ends just after he has fired the gun into his cheek. He is holding Marla's hand, watching from the window the collapse of a series of skyscraper office blocks that Tyler has wired for destruction, an ultimate act of urban terrorism that has a completely different impact after September 11th, 2001. The narrator however, *seems* to have escaped from Tyler—only a subliminal cut of a full-frontal male nude as the film draws to a close suggests that Tyler might still be around somewhere.

This refers back to one of Tyler's many part-time jobs, working as a projectionist in a movie theater where he occasionally splices single frames of pornography into family films. Tyler may be a "projection," but he is also the projectio*nist*, a further confusion of the internal and external doubles. The final subliminal cut suggests that Tyler exists no longer in the narrative but in the very fabric of the film: as the projectionist, he orchestrates events. Again, this is a subtle touch that is possible in the film and not in the book. Tyler is a visual and cinematic devil. Gil-Martin, who, the second time we meet him, is engrossed in a large book that looks like a bible, is a more literary and rhetorical devil, as is only appropriate since he is dealing with a society and an individual fascinated by the literal interpretation of the word. Tyler relies far more on the exploitation of the image.

Despite their generic differences, Tyler and Gil-Martin work in similar ways, and the very close parallels between specific stages of Robert's story and that of the narrator of *Fight Club* suggest parallel destructive processes. Reading *Fight Club* in the light of *Justified Sinner* also means rereading Hogg's novel in the light of *Fight Club*. The effect of this is to show how modern a novel *Justified Sinner* is, and to a certain extent to open up its interpretation. *Fight Club* shows that the dangers highlighted by Hogg are not restricted to a particular time or religious conviction. Rather, it suggests that idealism of any sort is open to corruption, and demonstrates the way in which idealism may blind the believer to its potential consequences. The absence of an explicitly religious aspect to *Fight Club* emphasizes the universality of the justified sinner's story. Fanatical religious belief is the context but not necessarily the cause of his downfall. Fanaticism takes many forms, and in *Fight Club* it is transformed into an impulse toward destruction for its own sake, spurred on by disenchantment and nihilism. The comparison of *Fight Club* with *Justified Sinner* shows how the discourse of fanaticism survives and transforms itself in different centuries and very different cultural milieus. Hogg's exploration of Robert's descent into irrationality, the emptiness of his life which he fills with fanatical belief, and the addictive nature of his relationship with Gil-Martin, would not be out of place in the urban wasteland of Palahniuk or Fincher.

Works Cited

Hogg, James. *The Private Memoirs and Confessions of a Justified Sinner*. London: Penguin Classics, 1987.

Sedgwick, Eve Kosofsky. "Murder Incorporated: Confessions of a Justified Sinner" in *Between Men: English Literature and Male Homosocial Desire*. New York: Columbia University Press, 1985.

Miyoshi, Masao. *The Divided Self: A Perspective on the Literature of the Victorians*. New York and London: New York University Press; University of London Press, 1969.

Nabokov, Vladimir. "The Strange Case of Dr. Jekyll and Mr. Hyde" in *Lectures on Literature*, Bowers, Fredson, ed. New York and London: Harcourt Brace, 1980.

Stevenson, Robert Louis. *The Strange Case of Dr. Jekyll and Mr. Hyde*. London: Penguin, 1994.

Tennant, Emma. *The Bad Sister*. London: Picador, 1979.

———. *Two Women of London: The Strange Case of Ms. Jekyll and Mrs. Hyde*. London: Faber and Faber, 1989.

The following essay is one of the top ten that made Metaphilm famous. Galvin P. Chow, who wrote this when he was an undergraduate at Haverford College in Pennsylvania, now teaches English in Japan. You can see his writings and musings (but don't call it a blog) at www.kindofcrap.com.

The Return of Hobbes

Galvin P. Chow

I n the film *Fight Club*, the real name of the protagonist (Edward Norton's character) is never revealed. Many believe the reason behind this anonymity is to give "Jack" more of an "everyman" quality. Do not be deceived. "Jack" is really Calvin from the comic strip *Calvin and Hobbes*. It's true. Norton portrays the grown-up version of Calvin, and Brad Pitt plays his imaginary pal Hobbes, reincarnated as Tyler Durden.

Part I: The Hobbes-Tyler Connection

Picture this: a hyper, self-absorbed child initially concocts an imaginary friend as the ideal playmate, to whom more realistic qualities soon become attributed. This phantasm becomes a completely separate personality, with his own likes, dislikes, and temperament—and the imaginer and the imagined clash and argue constantly, though remaining fast friends. This pattern continues to the point where the child begins to perceive what was originally mere fantasy to actually be *reality*.

Just as Calvin has an imaginary jungle-animal friend named Hobbes, whom everyone else believes to be nothing but a stuffed toy, "Jack" in *Fight Club* has an imaginary cool-guy friend named Tyler, whom no one but Jack can see.

In both cases, the entity that began as the ideal imaginary companion soon takes on a more realistic, three-dimensional quality. In other words, they become *real*. This is evident in that both Hobbes and Tyler also begin to function as scapegoats for their creators. Calvin often blames broken lamps and other assorted household mischief on Hobbes, and Jack is inclined to believe that fight club and other various anti-society mischief is brought about by Tyler. Calvin claims Hobbes pounces on him every day after school; Jack believes Tyler beats him up next to forty kilotons of nitroglycerin in a parking garage. The list goes on and on. The relationship between the two sets of friends is exactly the same. Is this mere coincidence?

Filling in the time gap between Calvin and Jack, we can imagine that the story goes something like this: Once Calvin reaches the hostile environment known as the seventh grade, the constant teasing from the other students and the frustrated concern of his parents finally become too much, and a reluctant, disillusioned Calvin is finally forced to grow up, or at least begin to. This decision is sealed by one of the hardest things young Calvin will ever have to do in his life: un-imagine Hobbes, an act which to Calvin is essentially no different from murder. After being Calvin's best friend for more than a decade, Hobbes is packed away in a box, or tossed carelessly into a garbage bag, perhaps even stuffed under the same bed that once contained so many monsters. This is all, of course, very painful for Calvin, so much so that he represses it all in shame. Little does Calvin suspect that while he is busy growing up, deciding what "dinette set defines him as a person," Hobbes is also maturing in the recesses of his mind, waiting to be unleashed.

It's worth noting that during these twenty or so years, Hobbes never bears a grudge against Calvin, nor does he wish any ill upon him. Hobbes, remembering the depth of their past friendship, does not hate Calvin, but rather hates the *society* that made Calvin put him away. Hobbes, residing in Calvin's mind, sees and experiences all that Calvin does—and truly despises all of it. He witnesses a bright, superbly imaginative kid (with a genius-level vocabulary) reduced to nothing more than another nameless cog. Fighting off the tears wept for his conventionalized pal, Hobbes resolves to set him free, paying special attention when Calvin idly looks up homemade-napalm recipes on the Internet.

Flash forward to the time frame depicted in *Fight Club*. Calvin/Jack has reached an all-time low. He has done everything society has told him to do, yet he is completely bereft of happiness. Hobbes, newly adjusted as "Tyler Durden" (after all, grown-up Calvin would no longer accept a jungle animal walking, talking, and eating canned tuna), reenters Calvin/Jack's life, determined to show Calvin everything he's done wrong, whether he likes it or not.

Tyler to Jack: "I look like you wanna look, I fuck like you wanna fuck, I'm smart, capable, and most importantly, I'm free in all the ways you wish you could be."

Calvin has always idolized Hobbes. In *Weirdos from Another Planet*, Calvin dresses up like a tiger and attempts to live in the woods. Like Hobbes, Tyler is cool, collected, and incredibly cerebral. Given this evidence, it is clear that Tyler is Hobbes reincarnated, after being trapped inside Calvin/Jack's brain for so many years.

Part II: Marla Singer—Avatar of Susie Derkins

Somewhere between the end of high school and the beginning of college, the uptight, grade-obsessed Susie Derkins loses her way. The pressure to get good grades, the relentless drive to succeed, simply becomes too much for her, and she snaps.

Free from the protective bonds of her parents' guidance and the bland safety of her suburban home, Susie loses her moral bearings entirely and sinks into a dark, seamy, grim world of sex, drugs, and eccentric Albert Einstein–like hair. Her transformation is so complete that she no longer even remotely resembles the upright citizen that her parents and society wanted her to be, so she changes her name.

Like Calvin, Susie has become a misfit, one of society's lost lambs. It is for this reason that she soon finds herself frequenting support groups such as "Remaining Men Together." Fate has brought her back to Calvin, whom she probably spurned back in junior high. But the two have changed so much that they no longer recognize each other!

The pink dress Marla wears in one scene slightly resembles something that Binky Betsy, Susie's favorite childhood doll, once wore—the same doll that Calvin stole and attempted to ransom. But while Calvin and Susie mostly teased and tortured each other as children, Hobbes was infatuated with the raven-haired beauty. Accordingly, Jack despises Marla, whereas Tyler takes an—*ahem*—sort of interest in her (one that is definitely inappropriate for the Sunday Funnies).

When we are first introduced to Marla, she is but a tumor on Jack's slowly deteriorating world. She is disenfranchised, morbid, socially apathetic—and Jack despises her because she is a mirror image of himself, his own female double. On the other hand, the unruly young Calvin hated Susie because she was his exact opposite: bright, obedient, demure. However, certain strips definitely indicated that Calvin had somewhat of a crush on Susie, and some even implied that Susie shared these latent feelings. But as a cootie-fearing grade-schooler, Calvin could only express these strange feelings through attention-getting antagonisms, such as constant snowballs to the head, ransoming her dolls—*and* through his separate, conveniently more mature other personality, Hobbes.

Unlike Calvin, Hobbes was never bashful about showing his affection for Susie. Calvin's imaginary tiger-friend called her a "cutie," wore swim jams to impress her ("Girls flip for guys in jams"), and even claimed he would betray their club's secret code if she gave him a tummy rub (which is one of the key differences between Tyler and Hobbes). Naturally, all of this confused and frustrated Calvin beyond words, even though Hobbes was really nothing more than a product of his own mind! And though Hobbes and Susie never consummated their love for one another (he's a stuffed tiger and she's a kid, you sicko!), this is, of course, the *exact same* deranged love triangle that appears between Jack, Tyler, and Marla—or at least it is a natural progression thereof. Perhaps Marla puts up with Jack/Tyler's apparent nonsense for so long because it's the sort of thing she became used to as a child. And perhaps, in the end, Jack finds solace in Marla because it's the exact connection he should've made long ago, in his suburban youth; a connection that might have saved them both.

Part III: G.R.O.S.S.—Precursor of Fight Club

When you boil it down, the fight club that Jack and Tyler start is really just an odd sort of boys' club—no ovaries allowed—where men can be men, and the so-called stronger of the sexes can take solace in the fact that, even in our politically correct times, some exclusivities of manhood still remain. (As a side note, imagine how much more controversy the movie would have generated if it involved scenes of men fighting women on equal ground!)

And clubs like this, of course, have their beginnings in backyards, tree houses, and garages all over America. Not surprisingly, Calvin started such a club when he was six years old. Just as Calvin, Hobbes, and Susie have dark future versions in Jack, Tyler, and Marla, G.R.O.S.S. (**G**et **R**id **O**f **S**limy girl**S**) is the childhood incarnation of fight club.

G.R.O.S.S. shares the following characteristics with fight club:

- Both have catchy names (although the "slimy" part of G.R.O.S.S. is redundant, otherwise it doesn't spell anything).
- Both are co-run by a friendless male and his imaginary companion (Calvin is Tyrant and Dictator-for-Life of G.R.O.S.S.; Hobbes is its President and First Tiger).
- Both are exclusively male organizations, although fight club's membership is considerably larger.
- All members of both organizations are very loyal.
- The leaders of both organizations constantly engage in fisticuffs (but only in G.R.O.S.S. does a member receive a demerit for biting).

- Both are supposedly very secretive (though Jack never tells his mother about fight club).
- At least one leader of both organizations is fond of giving speeches (though Calvin never uses the term "space monkey").
- G.R.O.S.S. and fight club both wreak havoc on their respective neighborhoods (though G.R.O.S.S.'s target is considerably more focused, i.e., Susie).

Clearly, the roots of fight club can be seen in G.R.O.S.S. Calvin shows his penchant in childhood for such male-oriented, destructive organizations. Also, just like cardboard-box time-machines and water-gun transmogrifiers, G.R.O.S.S. was likely created as an escape, a release—as, of course, was fight club.

Part IV: Moe Develops Karmic Bitch Tits

Robert "Moe" Paulson, Calvin's grade-school bully, became a six-time weightlifting champion, and somewhere along the line he developed large man boobs as a result of testicular cancer. This of course led him to his support group, where he was shocked to find Calvin.

Moe greatly regrets his bullying days, but, too ashamed to reveal his true identity to the man he bullied as a child, he instead offers his ample bosom for Calvin to cry on, as a measure of retribution.

Part V: The Root of Evil

Although we've already discussed of the fates of Calvin, Hobbes, Susie, and Moe, there are a couple of other important people from Calvin's life that are missing in *Fight Club*, people who are even more integral to his development (arguably) than Hobbes: his parents. Mr. . . . uhm . . . , and Mrs. . . . uh. . . . Okay, so they don't have names. But then again, there is no *need* to know them. Because in the comic strip, they're not supposed to be important characters in their own right. They only matter in regard to how Calvin is directly affected by them, an effect which, by the time of the film, doesn't seem to have been very positive. From what "Jack" mentions, he's not exactly close to his parents, particularly his dad, on whom he seems to pin many of his problems. And this matches perfectly with the relationship depicted in the comic, as well as with what happened afterward (as described in Part I).

Calvin's dad seems to have done quite a number on his son. As stated, it was probably at his urging that Calvin "grew up," that is, finally started to conform to society's rules, which meant the death of Hobbes. Of course, Calvin's father wasn't without his playful side— good-naturedly teasing Calvin at every opportunity—but perhaps this is why "Jack" resents him so much. Maybe after Jack reached the end of his dutiful journey only to find emptiness, he thought back to the day his father told him that the sun sets down somewhere in Arizona every night. "Maybe," thought Calvin, "maybe *all* of it has been just another one of Dad's cruel jokes."

In the bathtub scene in *Fight Club*, Jack and Tyler discuss their woeful parents. In this scene, crucial information is revealed, as well as some inconsistencies. Jack claims his father left when he was six (an age when Calvin's dad was obviously still around), but this statement is contradicted soon after, when Tyler mentions his own dad telling him to get married when he was thirty, to which Jack responds, "mine said that *too*." The self-pitying Jack is most likely seeking to garner additional sympathy from his newfound friend by making his childhood sound worse than it actually was.

But even more interesting is Tyler's hostility toward his father: When Jack asks Tyler who he would fight, if he could fight anyone, he answers, "I'd fight my father." But, since Tyler is only a figment of Jack's imagination, we can only assume he's referring to *Jack's* father. And while this hatred would only make sense, given that the two are sharing the same brain, why is it that Tyler seems to hate Jack's father even more intensely than Jack himself does? Maybe it's because Tyler hasn't forgotten who was ultimately responsible for the un-imagining that took place years before . . . maybe he's still not too happy about it . . . and maybe he's had the time to develop some pretty good ideas for revenge.

The role of Calvin's father in all this is no small one. Other than to "save" Calvin/Jack, it's entirely possible that Tyler's real motivation for taking down all of civilization is simply to get back at Calvin's father. For by destroying the society that forced Calvin into repressing Hobbes, he's also destroying the society that Calvin's father, after all, epitomizes.

Part VI: Calvin—"I Am Jack's Lost Youth"

Although the personality differences between Calvin in the comic strip and Calvin in the movie are pretty large, it can be explained as easily as taking Id and introducing him to Superego (Jack actually seems to have sort of a super-superego). Nearly all people go through the same thing when first confronted with the crushing grind of reality. But, as they say, the bigger they are, the harder they fall—and in terms of imagination and dreams, Calvin was a giant.

Still, it's not as though common traits between Calvin-Calvin and Jack-Calvin can't be identified at all. Besides a preference for imaginary friends over real ones, and an inability to express affection for girls, Calvin has never done well when forced to play by any sort of rules. Take, for instance, his utter inability to play any sort of organized sport, compared to his unbridled joy while playing the make-it-up-as-you-go-along Calvinball. Furthermore, even at age six Calvin never exactly thrived in stifling, authoritarian establishments (i.e., school), and he's had clashes with authority figures since the strip began (his parents, the doctor, his teacher, Rosalyn)—which actually may have planted the initial seeds for Tyler. Beyond that, his excellent vocabulary and eloquent way with words are still with him in the voiceover narration of *Fight Club*, and his rampant materialism, which started with mail-order propeller-beanies, ends with yin-yang-shaped tables. As for the differences, they can be credited to the demoralizing effect of reality.

In the end, Calvin's involvement with fight club and the return of Hobbes can be boiled down to two words: "personal responsibility." For although fight club and Project Mayhem were both mostly Tyler's doing, by the end of the movie, Jack readily accepts his own part of the blame, as Tyler is his creation. And by doing so, Jack also accepts responsibility for the undesirable condition of his own *life—*

his father may have pushed him, but Calvin himself was the one who chose to obey. It is through this newfound self-accountability that Calvin/Jack is able to take control of his own life at last. As skyscrapers flash and crumble in the background and blood oozes from the bullet hole in his head, Calvin says that he is "Ok." And we are apt to believe him.

Part VII: Conclusion

Calvin's world in the comic strip is pure, romanticized idealism, whereas in the movie he lives in gray, bleak reality. Within the safety of the panel, Calvin is perpetually six years old, terrible things can never happen, and no matter how crazy a stunt he pulls, everything always returns to the status quo. Because of this, our hero is free to do as he wishes, free to chase his dreams as wildly as he desires, and never have to worry about tomorrow because there essentially will never *be* one (unless it's part of a continuing storyline). This makes the reality of *Fight Club* all the bleaker, because it depicts what happens when you take someone weaned on dreams and limitless possibilities and jam him into a cramped cage confined by rules and regulations. It probably only took poor Calvin a few years in the adult world (or the growing-up world) to fully make the sad change.

This transition from gleeful Calvin to dull Jack is not uncommon: Little Nemo became a banker, Peter Pan became a lawyer, and Garfield was caught and butchered by the chef of a Chinese restaurant. (One exception is Charlie Brown, who from all indications was mentally middle-aged at the time of his birth.)

The moral of the story is that reality bites, kiddies. Calvin and Hobbes in *Fight Club* are proof of this sad, sad truth.

Discussion Questions

1. In the film, Calvin and Hobbes actually reversed many personality traits as Jack and Tyler. Is it possible that Calvin is the personality that got repressed and Hobbes is the one that did the "growing up"?

2. Tyler wears a fur coat near the end of the movie. What is the significance of this garment, given his past incarnation as a jungle animal?

3. If Calvin really wanted to change things, why didn't he just dust off his old cardboard-box time-machine and hop in?

4. After the end of *Fight Club*, when Calvin realizes he's effectively killed Hobbes twice now, do you really think he'll still be "Ok"?

Vox Day is a writer and Internet superintelligence hosted on a European server. He is a former martial artist and the author of numerous books, games, and electronic dance hits. His most recent book is *The Irrational Atheist: Dissecting the Unholy Trinity of Dawkins, Harris, and Hitchens* (BenBella, 2008).

In this piece, Day takes on both the physics of fighting and the homo-erotic "subtext" of the novel.

The Physics of *Fight Club*

There is a savage joy in violence. The secret of the success of *Fight Club* is its acceptance of that basic and uncomfortable truth, which is as well known to every martial artist, gang member, and football hooligan as it is completely alien to the sedentary sort of middle-aged individuals favored by those who publish novels. For as men have known since long before the Colosseum's sands were first soaked with blood, there is no adrenaline rush so great as the moment when two men put one another to the physical test.

Fight Club is a fascinating little book that not only embraced that truth, but in doing so, translated surprisingly well to the cinematic medium. This should probably not have been surprising, given that the author's witch's brew of male fury and raw but stylized violence is almost perfectly suited for that male audience which so enjoys the cinematic adventures of Bruce Lee, Jean-Claude van Damme, Jackie Chan, and a host of other aggressively oriented male leads. The combination of that visceral appeal with the brilliant casting of a ripped and shirtless Brad Pitt for the ladies, and Hollywood hit status was all but assured.

When viewed from a technical perspective, *Fight Club* is nearly as absurd as any *wuxia* extravaganza featuring aerial acrobatics and mad dashes through the treetops, whereas from a psychological perspective, it is impressively accurate. To the combat-aware reader, the book raises the interesting question of how the author could have gotten the latter so right and the former so wrong.

Fight Club subscribes to the common conventional fiction that it is not the size of the dog in the fight that matters, but rather the size of the fight in the dog. Although in *Fight Club* terms, this might be better described as the size of the proverbial canine's violent sociopathy. As with most aphorisms, there is an element of truth to this; all things being equal, the tougher individual will usually prevail. But outside the formalized structure of the boxing ring, all things are very seldom equal.

The most basic truth of unarmed combat is that $F = M \times A$: Force equals Mass times Acceleration. Since Force is the measurement of what is smashing into your face and is the primary variable determining exactly what the effect of that blow will be, it is very important to understand the significance of this equation. Mass, being a function of size, indicates that a larger individual will usually pack a more powerful punch than a smaller one. Usually, but not always.

Because Acceleration is just as important as Mass. Acceleration comes in two forms, the first being the speed with which the individual can deliver the blow. This can come from natural speed (given a choice, always elect to get punched by a marathon runner, not a sprinter), or from the perfected technique that is a product of training. The second form of Acceleration is the relative motion of two bodies, which is to say, if you are moving toward the puncher at the moment the punch arrives, it will hurt significantly more than if you are moving away from him.

When these elements all come together, they result in the perfect storm that is the instantaneous knockout. I once made the mistake of getting overconfident and attempted to go inside on a 6'5", 260-pound fighter who was slow, inflexible, and therefore almost helpless at kicking range. His Mass was obviously superlative, however, and I unwisely granted him the benefit of Acceleration by moving straight in toward him at full speed. The multiplication of the two forces was such that a simple defensive jab on his part left me waking up on the concrete floor, wondering what had happened and where I was.

The second fundamental truth of unarmed combat is that evasion is everything. This is why blocks are given the same importance as strikes; indeed, the famous "wax-on, wax-off" from *The Karate Kid* is not only better known than any exotic attacking technique, but is genuinely part of the basic repertoire of any traditionally trained martial artist.

At the basic level, evasive options are limited. But for the trained fighter, there are a whole host of techniques at one's disposal, including oblique movement, gap management, arrhythmic timing, destructive blocks, and simultaneous offense-defense. All these tactics and more have been developed to allow the fighter to avoid the direct application of Force to his body; indeed, the martial arts are customarily divided into the hard style, wherein the opponent's Force is met with Force, and the soft style, wherein one seeks to use the opponent's Force against him.

Kali, for example, is a Filipino hard style. Its brutal destructive blocks make heavy use of the knees and elbows, so that in the place of a traditional "wax-off" block designed to deflect a blow with the forearm, the arm is flexed and the point of the elbow is used to block the incoming strike instead. The ease with which the elbow can break an ankle or a wrist makes delivering a blow nearly as dangerous as receiving a direct one; even a partial block will sting an opponent and make him very wary of attempting another attack.

Kung fu, on the other hand, is the classic soft style. By redirecting the incoming Force and allowing it to flow past him, a soft response allows the martial artist to do things he could not hope to do using only his own Force. Soft styles are particularly effective in dealing with the conventional brute force attacks of the sort seen in the *Fight Club* film, for while it is extremely difficult to put an opponent in a neck-breaking lock by taking the offensive, it is very easy indeed if the attacker is so obliging as to dive forward and attempt to tackle one at the waist.*

Fight Club fighting was mostly hard style, albeit of the untrained variety, which prides itself on winning through attrition and outlasting the other guy. And this brings up what may be the most intriguing and dichotomous aspect of *Fight Club*, for while both the literary and cinematic depictions of the actual fighting were absurd in regard to the length—twenty minutes!—and nature of the fights, the author did an excellent job of describing the psychological effects of fighting on the fighter.

But first, the absurdities. Without artificial restraints, when there are no rules, most fights are concluded in a matter of seconds rather than minutes once the action begins. This is especially true when the fighters are trained, as the human body's ability to deal out damage tends to exceed its capacity to withstand it. The image of the bloody warriors fighting to the point of exhaustion and beyond is a Hollywood cliché; in reality, the fight is usually settled as soon as one fighter's defenses are penetrated, and matters speed quickly to an end.

---

*You merely pull your legs back, riding the tackler back with the force of his momentum while allowing your upper body to be driven forward over the tackler's shoulder. Drop your left arm under his right armpit and your right in the gap between his head and left shoulder. As the tackler continues to drive forward in an attempt to take you off your feet, (which is no problem, so long as you have the lock in place before you go down on top of him), grab his jaw with your right hand and pull up while snaking your left hand over the top of his neck and taking hold of your right wrist. Pull upward to tighten the lock as needed. If you hear a loud cracking sound, then you've pulled too hard and should probably contact an attorney. This may sound complicated but it actually takes around two to three seconds tops and can usually be completed before the tackler stops pushing forward or has any idea that he is in danger.

The popular cinematic vision of a back-and-forth battle, wherein one fighter has the advantage first, then loses it as the other fighter valiantly demonstrates his toughness by battling back, owes rather more to sports such as boxing and even basketball than it does to the martial arts. Fighting is a surprisingly hierarchical endeavor, as one fighter who can beat another fighter will almost always beat that other fighter, even if they are relatively evenly matched. The balance of a fight is rather like that of a snowball perched precariously on the top of a hill. It may wobble back and forth initially, but once it begins rolling downhill, it seldom stops and reverses course uphill in order to go down the other side.*

If the fights in *Fight Club* themselves are somewhat fantastic, the portrayal of the mental state behind them is not. The scene in the bathroom at the office was what arrested my attention and made me realize that *Fight Club* was truly something unusual, as it perfectly captured the alienation of the fighter from a society that thoroughly disapproves of physical violence. As for the constant measuring of every man who passes by as a potential opponent, the mental matchup that takes place every time a man crosses another man's path is an instinctual habit in which every fighter automatically engages.

There is a silent arrogance inside every fighter, a quiet contempt for those who are afraid to do what he does and yet still dare to judge him for his blackened eyes, his bandaged hands, and the marks that remind them that not all the world is soft and fat and weak. While physics makes the fighter, what makes *Fight Club* fascinating is the glimpse it gives us of what lies beneath the civilized mask.

The Flamers of *Fight Club*

At the time that I read *Fight Club*, I had not heard of its author. But before I finished the first chapter, I was entirely convinced that whoever

---

*This isn't to say that whoever gets the first punch in wins, as most fighters can shake off a single lucky or unexpected blow, but rather, whoever gets in the first three strikes in uninterrupted succession is quite likely to be the victor.

he might be, he wasn't particularly interested in women, sexually or otherwise. And between the first page and the last, I read nothing that caused me to change my mind—rather the opposite, actually.

One cannot really say that *Fight Club* has a homosexual subtext, because the concept of a literary subtext generally implies some degree of subtlety, and at the very least demands an absence of screaming obviousness flaunting itself in the reader's face with all the discretion of a Sydney pride parade. Consider the very first scene of the book, wherein one man is thrusting a hard cylindrical object into another man's mouth:

> That old saying, how you always kill the one you love, well, look, it works both ways. With a gun stuck in your mouth and the barrel of the gun between your teeth, you can only talk in vowels. . . . Tyler and me at the edge of the roof, the gun in my mouth, I'm wondering how clean this gun is.

No sooner does this oral performance come to an end than the second chapter begins with the reader discovering the protagonist in the massive arms of Big Bob, in which he has apparently been finding weekly release for two years. In only a few sparse pages, by sharing the loving relationships between two different pairs of men with the reader, the author manages to introduce him to two of the classic fascinations of the homosexual community, Death and the unending Search for the Father.

Big Bob also introduces the theme of gender confusion, what with his missing testicles and bitch tits. More importantly, the basement of the support group meeting in the Trinity Episcopal Church foreshadows the coming activities of the club that dare not speak its name, as pairs of men cling together "the way wrestlers stand, locked" and exchange bodily fluids. In this early case the fluid is tears, later it will be blood and sweat, and in both cases they metaphorically represent an altogether different substance.

There are other semiotic clues lurking amidst the gatherings of dying men, but perhaps the most telling symbol can be found in the support group scene: the protagonist's inability to perform and find the release he is seeking in the presence of a woman. Her sex defiles "the one real thing" in his life, the thing he needs, and his immediate reaction to her very being is a combination of hatred, disgust, and fear. It just doesn't get much more gay than that.

Unless of course you count the subsequent description of a slippery red penis, towering four stories over the unsuspecting heads of a movie audience. It serves as a markedly apt metaphor, both for the way in which many fans of *Fight Club* remain oblivious to the fact that it is a screaming, panting, writhing ode to the custom of men having sex with other men and the way in which an attachment to this custom tends to supersede all other aspects of individual self-identification.

"You Aren't Your Name. You Aren't Your Family"

In *Among the Thugs*, Bill Buford's 1990 book chronicling his eight years dabbling in European football hooliganism, Buford describes a bizarre scene in an English nightclub wherein the drunken ruffians ripped their shirts off and jumped madly up and down to heavy industrial music while packed in tight against one another. He found this activity to be weirdly homoerotic, considering the overwhelmingly straight tendencies of the soccer thugs.

But the hooligans' activities were always out in the open; indeed, they were often police-escorted and televised. The secretive nature of *Fight Club*, on the other hand, especially its First Rule, is rather more reminiscent of the notorious decree of the U.S. military: "Don't ask, don't tell." Moreover, it would take a truly superficial reader indeed to fail to note the glaring similarities between the fight clubs gathering anonymously in dark places while trying to stay out of trouble with the police and the shady, quasi-illegal bathhouses where gay men have trolled for sex for decades.

> Because I'm Tyler Durden and you can kiss my ass, I register to fight every guy in the club that night. Fifty fights. One fight at a time. No shoes. No shirts.

But no shortage of "service." Given that Tyler is one of the least risk-averse characters ever to inhabit a novel, one can safely conclude that there will be no condoms either in this climactic gang-bang. In a world without metaphor, surely this book would have been published as *Fuck Club*.

Although the motif of violence is enthralling, it is the homosexual themes that provide *Fight Club* with the haunting quality that truly sets it apart. Without them, and without what they appear to reveal about the author's own sense of being an outcast from mundane straight civilization, neither the book nor the film would be as emotionally powerful as they are.

The disturbing note on which the book ends is altogether fitting, combining as it does the contempt of the fighter with the alienation of the flamer. And yet, notwithstanding the way in which these two diverse elements worked surprisingly well in producing an intriguing novel, one remains rather skeptical that this is an alchemic formula that can be expected to make something better out of the world.

To paraphrase the great English philosophers, gay men lurking in cellars distributing fluids is no basis for a civilization.

In this piece, which was originally published on Metaphilm, Chris Landis argues that *Fight Club* is a smart new twist on the classic Greek tragedy, with Jack as a modern-day Oedipus and Tyler Durden as his father Laius. Landis lives in Ohio and works as a financial advisor (perfect for interpreting the philosophical aspects of film). Landis has several essays on Metaphilm and he loves birthday parties.

Tyler Durden Is a M*therf#cker

Chris Landis

The Story of Oedipus—On the Short

In the tale of Oedipus, Laius, the ruler of Thebes, sends his son away to be killed after an oracle tells Laius that his son will someday kill him. The child is spared, however, and given to the ruler of Corinth. The ruler and his wife are unable to have children, so they raise Oedipus as their own, never telling him of his adoption. Years later, Oedipus is going off to seek his fortune when he learns of a prophecy that says he will kill his father and marry his mother. So Oedipus heads in the opposite direction of Corinth, the home of the family that raised him, because as far as he knows, the people who rule Corinth are his natural parents and going to the city of Thebes will ensure his family's safety. As Oedipus is traveling to Thebes, he encounters Laius and, unaware that the man is his natural father, kills him. Oedipus then settles in Thebes and takes the widow Jocasta, who he doesn't know is his mother, for his wife. Finally, Oedipus discovers that the man he killed years before was his father when Jocasta announces that the man Oedipus killed was her husband and therefore Oedipus is her son. Stricken with guilt, Oedipus's mother hangs herself and Oedipus blinds himself with her dress-pins.

The Prophecy

As with the story of Oedipus, *Fight Club* begins with a prophecy. The film starts with its final scene, promising a future that is sure to come. The storyline then moves back in time so that Jack, who is also the narrator, can describe the events that lead to the movie's opening scene.

"I Am Jack's Broken Heart"

Jack's unhappiness is the catalyst that seems to drive the events that allow this strange story to unfold. Jack, like many people, is trying to fill his hollow, empty life with material possessions and consumerism. Ultimately deriving no joy from this lifestyle, Jack stumbles upon a support group for testicular cancer; this meeting is where Jack meets Bob. "Bob had bitch tits" and is "a cancer survivor." This scene is important. The hug that Bob and Jack share allows Jack to enjoy the nonsexual embrace of a huge man that is the proportionate equivalent of a father hugging a child. Significantly, Bob's bitch tits allow him to offer the physical characteristics of both a mother and a father in one person. Jack is blissful. The next scene shows Jack in bed.

> JACK (VOICEOVER): Babies don't sleep this well.

Tyler Durden Is Psychological Aspirin

Jack is in pain, but he doesn't know exactly why. Many lines point to Jack's lack of a father's love, guidance, and approval. Jack's father left when Jack was a boy.

Tyler Durden is the solution Jack's subconscious creates to deal with that pain. Like aspirin, Tyler's role is to find the pain and fix it.

Tyler has few inhibitions, and his view on society and life is based on a different set of values than that to which Jack is accustomed. As Tyler says to Jack, "You were looking for a way to change your life. You could not do this on your own. All the ways you wished you could be . . . that's me! I look like you wanna look, I fuck like you wanna fuck, I'm smart, capable, and most importantly, I'm free in all the ways that you are not."

Tyler becomes, for Jack and the other "space monkeys," a substitute father. Tyler teaches Jack and the others a new set of acceptable behaviors, including how to fight. Tyler provides shelter for all of them, teaches them that material possessions begin to own the owner. Tyler informs them that they are not going to be rock stars and millionaires, and Tyler teaches them how to make soap.

Toward the end of the film, however, Tyler disappears:

> JACK (VOICEOVER): First my father leaves me, now Tyler. I'm all alone. I am Jack's Broken Heart.

"If I Had a Tumor, I'd Name It Marla"

Jack's subconscious also creates Tyler as a way in which to deal with Marla Singer. Marla Singer is Jack's Jocasta. She represents the woman that Jack cannot love, or delusionally believes he isn't permitted to love, but who loves him nonetheless. Marla is strange, dirty ("needs a wash"), and neurotic, but she is consistently there for Jack and continues to reach out to him regardless of how he treats her.

Jack is unhappy because he doesn't have his father's love, but he never mentions his mother. We assume he was raised by his mother, but it seems Jack wasn't able to accept or be satisfied by only his mother's love. When Marla offers unconditional caring for Jack, I think he is unable to process the emotion and subconsciously categorizes her as his mother or mother-analogue. And if she is his mother or a mother substitute, he cannot engage her sexually—but Tyler can. After all, in Jack's mind, a mother and father are supposed to be together.

> JACK (VOICEOVER): I'm six years old again, passing messages between my parents.

When Tyler confronts Jack about his relationship with Marla, Jack is repulsed at the idea of a sexual relationship with her:

> TYLER: You know what I mean, you fucked her.
>
> JACK: No, I didn't.
>
> TYLER: Never?
>
> JACK: No.
>
> TYLER: You're not into her, are you?
>
> JACK: No, God, not at all.
>
> JACK (VOICEOVER): I am Jack's raging bile duct.
>
> TYLER: You're sure? You can tell me.
>
> JACK: Believe me, I'm sure.
>
> JACK (VOICEOVER): Put a gun to my head and paint the walls with my brains.

Who wouldn't have that reaction when accused of having lustful thoughts about his own mother?

A Truth Too Awful to Bear

Jack believes he has safely separated himself from the possibility of a relationship with Marla, just as Oedipus believed by traveling in the opposite direction of his home in Corinth that he had safely avoided the prophecy that foretold he would kill his father and marry his mother. The irony was that traveling in the opposite direction toward Thebes was actually a necessary step before Oedipus could fulfill the prophecy. The happy little nuclear family Jack constructs in *Fight Club* includes a similar irony: Jack, as Tyler, actually does become involved with Marla without knowing it. Tyler and Marla have the relationship that Jack cannot have, but Tyler is Jack, and once Jack realizes that he has been living a second existence through Tyler, he also realizes that he has been having sex with Marla, his mother.

After Oedipus realizes that he has killed his father and has been having sex with his mother, he blinds himself for what he has done. But when Jack becomes aware of the double life he has led, *Fight Club* diverges from the Oedipus tale in that Jack is surprised but not bothered by the relationship he has had with Marla. In fact, after this realization about his double life, Jack shows concern for Marla for the first time and sends her out of town so she will be safe. Jack is suddenly thinking more clearly.

However, Jack does travel a path similar to Oedipus's in that, after realizing what he/Tyler has done, he takes responsibility for his actions and attempts to turn himself in to the police. Unfortunately, they are also corrupted by Tyler's influence and so, after Jack escapes from the police in an effort to thwart Project Mayhem, he takes the only action he thinks is possible: he kills Tyler. Of course, since he is Tyler, this is actually an (unsuccessful) attempt to take his own life. This final scene also harkens to the Oedipus myth's conclusion, where Oedipus blinded himself because he could not face the truth. The irony is that after Jack has shot himself and killed Tyler, he is able to see more clearly. He now seems to not require his father or Tyler or anyone else; he is able to love Marla and accept her love in return.

If You Act Now, You Get These Additional Insights

BONUS COMMENT FOR OUR PLATINUM MEMBERS

The film seems to comment on the problems in a society where children are raised by a single parent and a color television. Unhappiness ensues when children believe that purchasing things will soothe their pain, because that same philosophy will follow them into adulthood:

> JACK: There's always that. I don't know, it's just . . . when you buy furniture, you tell yourself: that's it, that's the last sofa I'm gonna need. No matter what

else happens, I've got that sofa problem handled. I had it all. I had a stereo that was very decent, a wardrobe that was getting very respectable. I was so close to being complete.

BONUS COMMENT II

An argument could be made that the destructive and anachronistic elements of the film were a cry for attention. Playing by the rules, acquiring things, having a "good" job—none of these things worked for Jack. Perhaps as the delusional Tyler, Jack does an ethical one-eighty in hopes that his great act, Project Mayhem, will gain the attention he seeks.

BONUS COMMENT III

The story of Oedipus ends as Thebes is overcome with plague and disease. Oedipus promises to save his city, but the city's problems were a curse for the sins Oedipus had committed. Oedipus, no matter how hard he tried, was unable to escape his own fate. Tyler's (Jack's) actions destroy the credit bureaus and are intended to destroy civilization as we know it. Jack is unable to stop the events that Tyler (Jack) set in motion, and the credit card companies are destroyed. His actions are his sins and his sins are the curse.

A counter-argument: The film seems to direct us in believing the credit card companies, consumerism, and the typical American way of life are already diseased, and if this is the case then Jack's action are not sinful but virtuous. Since this film is a narrative piece, we are seeing things through Jack/Tyler's eyes, and we can safely assume Jack is insane; his perception of what is diseased and what is decent is tainted. The final act is terrorism and the end cannot justify the means, damnit.

Read Mercer Schuchardt is the founder and publisher of Metaphilm (www.metaphilm.com), a film interpretation Web site. He teaches communication to undergraduates.

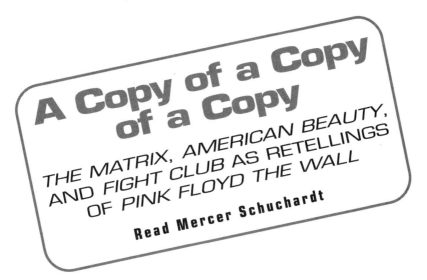

A Copy of a Copy of a Copy
THE MATRIX, AMERICAN BEAUTY, AND FIGHT CLUB AS RETELLINGS OF PINK FLOYD THE WALL
Read Mercer Schuchardt

1999 was the year that everything changed. It was the year the dot.com bubble burst, a year after the Internet became a mass medium, and the year *Entertainment Weekly* said all the rules of cinema were reinvented. It was a year of overmediation in one medium and reflection upon that very fact in another. *Entertainment Weekly* was calling it the year that changed everything in reference to new special-effects techniques in *The Matrix* and new narrative techniques in films like *Being John Malkovich* and *Run Lola Run*. But it was also, in retrospect, a year of incredible movie-making that included films like *Fight Club*, *American Beauty*, and *Magnolia*. I think that no small part of that cinematic greatness came from a merging of two forces that had been gathering steam for the previous century: 1) the increasing tendency of cinema, as both a medium and as a physical environment, to replace the cathedral in its place, purpose, and meaning in daily life, and 2) the increasing fear, loneliness, and alienation that Americans felt as a result of their increased wealth, technology, and supremacy in the post–Cold War order. I believe these two trends collided to create a cinema of profoundly honest spiritual yearning that was surprising, beautiful, and powerful. You could almost feel how powerfully embarrassing it was when, not two years later, the teen-angst satire *Not Another Teen Movie* created a Ricky Fitts (from *American Beauty*) parody character dubbed "The Beautiful Weirdo." The parody character was necessary because Ricky Fitts had been a *little too beautiful*, a little too honest, and in retrospect many felt like it had to be gotten over quickly. An alternate reaction was the near-instant commodification of the spiritually yearning movie formula, which produced such transcendent clunkers as J.Lo.'s *Angel Eyes*, among others.

But still a deeper trend ran through many of these films: Instead of a generic spiritual search that the protagonists were put into, three films stood out as particularly revealing in their willingness to address the specific historical moment of our spiritual crisis as it intersected with the family, with mass media, and with gender roles. In order of their appearance, *The Matrix*, *American Beauty*, and *Fight Club* (released between April and October 1999) all dealt in some way with the following three themes: overmediation, fatherlessness, and homosexuality. These three movies both articulate these themes and present them as intricately but often subtextually interconnected. Ironically, these three films also have something profoundly familiar in them when compared to Roger Water's 1979 classic, *Pink Floyd The Wall*, made into a film by Alan Parker in 1982. If cultural texts come and go like fashion, it was almost as if the three authors of the 1999 films produced their most creative work by unintentionally recreating their favorite movie from adolescence. All three films, like *The Wall*, had phenomenal soundtracks. All three films, like *The Wall*, showed a man fighting a system against which he had no control but toward which he felt incredible rage and anger. And all three films, like *The Wall*, ultimately dealt with the fact that it was not Big Brother, but rather "big mother" who was watching you, and presented the world as a system in which the psychosocial and psychosexual consequences of fatherlessness are played out to the nth degree in the life of the male protagonist. Each film has its own take on the subject, but in every instance the male protagonist has to fight physically against an overfeminized system as a key to achieving his identity. From a media effects point of view, these films are all not merely fictional manifestations of Neil Postman's 1992 thesis in *Technopoly*—that culture had surrendered to technology—but to the idea that the feminine image had so replaced the masculine word that men were beginning to feel effeminate as a result. That the result was either homosexuality, rage, or a combination of the two in the lives of the authors or the protagonists, is telling. A culture-wide technological conditioning of homosexual inclinations, predicated on the absent father and the domineering mother in the form of mass media, may partially explain why Chuck Palahniuk's *Fight Club* was so popular. From a marketing point of view, writing a gay novel for a straight audience is a sure way to lose 90 percent of the market, *unless the market comes from a culture that has already been feminized.* As Weezer sang, "Everyone's a little bit gay," and so the story strikes the audience as normal, or even documentary-like, in its presentation of gender and gender roles.

In *Fight Club* and *The Matrix*, the protagonist is a single, white, male, urban professional at or around age thirty. In *American Beauty*, the protagonist is a married father, aged forty-two, but he is also accompanied by a secondary lead male character in the form of Ricky Fitts, the teenage son of Marine Colonel Fitts, the new neighbors of Lester Burnham's family in suburban New Jersey. So immediately, we are watching movies about Generation X, the post-boomer generation who were too young to serve in Vietnam and whose lives were largely untouched by any horrors larger than media spectacles and tragedies from space shuttle disasters to the roughly once-a-year horror of the nineties from Waco to Oklahoma City to TWA Flight 800 to the Unabomber to Columbine. *Fight Club* makes specific reference to this ongoing sense of malaise when comparing luck: Tyler Durden says to Jack after his apartment blows up, "It could be worse: you could have had your penis cut off and thrown out the window of a moving car." This reference to Lorena Bobbit, and the emasculation of her husband John on the one-year anniversary of her abortion, makes it clear that the film is subtextually about the emotional and psychological emasculation at the hands of either a woman or a highly feminized system. One of the teaser posters for *Fight Club* was simply a giant-text headline that says, "Wash your feminine side clean off." This becomes the dominant background metaphor against which all three male characters in all three films struggle. In *The Wall*, as the film progresses, we see the link between the smothering mother of Pink, whose father died in the war, and the wall of social isolation and alienation built up brick by brick by endless consumer choices that serve as distractions from life's more pressing realities. Interestingly, as the animated portions of the film take over, the Wall itself becomes symbolized by the mother, by feminine flowers that morph into ravenous female genitalia, and these are in turn analogized into the endless array of consumer products. The song "What Shall We Do Now?" accompanies this animated wall sequence with these words:

> What shall we use to fill the empty spaces?
> Where waves of hunger roar?
> Shall we set out across the sea of faces
> In search of more and more applause?
> Shall we buy a new guitar?
> Shall we drive a more powerful car?
> Shall we work straight through the night?
> Shall we get into fights?
> Leave the lights on?
> Drop bombs?
> Do tours of the east?
> Contract diseases?
> Bury bones?
> Break up homes?
> Send flowers by phone?
> Take to drink?
> Go to shrinks?
> Give up meat?
> Rarely sleep?
> Keep people as pets?
> Train dogs?
> Race rats?
> Fill the attic with cash?

Bury treasure?
Store up leisure?
But never relax at all
With our backs to the wall.

In *American Beauty*, Lester Burnham (Kevin Spacey) makes an explicit reference to Pink Floyd when visiting Ricky Fitts's home. He speaks almost directly to the Pink Floyd imagery in the song above when he says to Carolyn, "This isn't life, it's just stuff!" in reference to their four-thousand-dollar sofa. And not coincidentally, the filmic image of human figures in front of walls is one of the recurring visual motifs each time a significant change happens in *American Beauty*. These are 1) Lester smoking pot against a white wall with Ricky outside at night, 2) the white plastic bag against the bricks of the red wall that is "the most beautiful thing" Ricky Fitts has ever filmed, and 3) Lester's red blood against the white tiles of the kitchen wall after he has been murdered at the end of the movie. Thus, the wall in *American Beauty* implodes inward on the mind of Lester Burnham—whose sacrificial death atones for his own sins and the audience's projected sins—and releases the audience to see life as he sees it, with the inability to feel "anything but gratitude for every single moment of [his] stupid little life."

Lester Burnham, who is trapped in a loveless marriage to Carolyn, must struggle against his wife who keeps not only his "dick in a Mason jar," but who also keeps everything in their life perfect, static, and spiritually dead. The screenwriter Alan Ball shows us this by associating Carolyn with the death of plants in the film, and by extension with her death-like effect on any element that is wild in nature. The film's opening introduction to Carolyn's character shows her snipping off a rose just below its stem with a fantastically glazed look in her eyes while her husband's voiceover monotones, "See the way her gardening shears match her clogs: that's no accident." The rose, of course, is the American Beauty, a species grown to be visibly flawless and perfect, except that it tends to rot from underneath and within (and produces no smell, I'm told)—Ball's restraint in not revealing this detail within the script itself makes it all the more delicious when we learn it later on, because it confirms all that his film has been saying—that a life led this way may as well be cultivating plastic flowers as anything real. Carolyn later discusses the root formation of a tree that the old neighbor has let grow into her yard, which is one reason she cut it down and why Lester secretly believes they moved out of the neighborhood. Finally, Carolyn is shown with a lesbian couple trying to sell the house when they complain that the backyard is not a tropical jungle, that it doesn't have nearly the plant life they had been led to believe it had, and Carolyn weakly suggests, "I've got some tiki torches in the back of the car. . . ."

Under these conditions, the viewer is encouraged to be more sympathetic to Lester's nonetheless pathetic condition in slavering over his daughter's teenage girlfriend—Lester fantasizes about Angela as the sexual essence of a rose, who bathes in roses, and who kisses him so that afterward, he pulls a rose petal out of his mouth. In the original script Lester does in fact have sex with Angela, but in the final version he only barely resists the temptation upon discovering that despite her horny cheerleader vulgarities, she is in fact a virgin.

Alan Ball, the screenwriter of *American Beauty*, so perfectly documents the dysfunction of middle-class suburban perfectionism that one wonders if another, straight screenwriter could have had the aesthetic distance from which to perceive these hypocrisies. If it means anything that Alan Ball (*American Beauty*), Chuck Palahniuk (*Fight Club*), and at least one of the Wachowski Brothers (*The Matrix*) are not completely heterosexual, then it may simply be confirmation of the truism that a cultural outsider is often the best one for analyzing the inside of a culture. As Marshall McLuhan pointed out, we don't know who discovered water, but we know it wasn't a fish.

For Tyler Durden in *Fight Club*, the question is not one of an emasculating mother, but of an absent father. In the course of the film, before we discover that Jack and Tyler are the same character, the two of them discuss their respective fathers, who, in hindsight, are of course the same person:

> JACK: I never really knew my father.
>
> TYLER: Me neither.

> JACK: My father divorced my mother when I was
> about six, moved to another town, married another
> woman, and started having kids with her.
>
> TYLER: Fucker's setting up franchises.

Later in the same conversation, Tyler says, "We're a generation of men raised by women: I'm wondering if another woman is really the answer we need." The two men go on to form fight club, which is essentially a form of primal scream therapy in which men vent their rage at the world (and their own failures) by physically pummeling each other. But throughout the film there is a phenomenal amount of homosexual subtext and inside jokes, from Tyler and Jack's Ozzie-and-Harriet relationship to Jack's dildo in his luggage to various clues that Marla Singer (and by extension, Jack's heterosexuality), is also a figment of his imagination. That *Fight Club* was originally a novel by Chuck Palahniuk, and that all of Palahniuk's work deals with themes of homosexuality, are not surprising once you've read it, and especially not once Mr. Palahniuk himself came out publicly in 2003. But it is a complex and particularly honest portrayal, if Camille Paglia is correct in her assessment that a large part of explaining the rise in male homosexuality in the last three decades can be directly attributed to the divorce rate and the subsequent rise in fatherlessness. But part and parcel of this feminization is the willingness to feed at the teat of consumer culture, and Tyler Durden soon evolves fight club into Project Mayhem, in which he takes on *Adbusters*-style culture jamming techniques as a means of social upheaval, rants and raves against consumerism and television, and ultimately attempts to blow up credit card buildings in order to restart the human race at the beginning by erasing the debt record and presumably making everyone truly equal again.

For Thomas Anderson, the protagonist in *The Matrix*, the problem is manifold. His storyline gives him neither a mother nor a father, and yet in his technological dystopia that he comes to learn is not science fiction but actual reality, he learns that he is in fact a baby inside a large pod, and that this system that is his true "parent." That the Matrix is meant to symbolize the feminine is evidenced by the fact that the word "matrix" itself is Latin for *womb*, and by the camera angle at which we first encounter the protagonist. We first see Mr. Anderson in an overhead shot asleep inside his home cubicle that has been arranged in an ovular shape. He is surrounded by his computer and his stereo, with his words, music, and images flickering by electronically around him as he sleeps, blissfully unaware of how profound this mediated reality parallels the true metaphysical nature of the world he is about to be introduced to. The constant electronic hum of mass media and communication technologies, from music to telephone to Internet searches, indicates that in his relationship to mass media, Anderson has become infantilized. For the Matrix is a strange fulfillment of both Huxley's and Orwell's warnings about the nature of a government-enforced totalitarian future. As Neil Postman saw it in *Amusing Ourselves to Death*, it was Huxley and not Orwell who got it right: We would be enslaved by what we loved far faster and easier than by what we feared. In the world of *The Matrix*, the citizens are largely happy but passive consumers of the corporate-entertainment complex who do not question the nature or legitimacy of its existence. Morpheus leads a crew of "known terrorists" in fighting this system, and in killing as many agents of the system as possible. Neo is essentially a spiritual orphan in this brave new world, and his ultimate lesson is that it is he who must cut the umbilical cord to a media matrix that would forever seek to keep him infantilized in the simple creation and satisfaction of exclusively carnal desire in electronic culture. In freeing himself, he becomes the film's savior figure, and then offers others the chance to free themselves. What is significant is that while the agents and enemies in the film are almost all played by men (representing various forces of the law), these men are ultimately protecting a black widow's nest of incubation. At the same time, *The Matrix* counterbalances this gendered enemy of a dominatrix with the all-knowing wisdom of the Oracle, a black female character whose role is to tell Neo his ultimate destiny. And while Neo's sexuality is not questioned in the film, it is worth noting that he is played in style and manner as a very androgynous male, while his female heroine is played by an equally androgynous female. Visually, he seems to be a very feminized man while Trinity is a very masculinized woman, and the film's sequels make it clear that the directors see that gender is as much of a choice and a cultural performance to be played as it is a sexual identity at birth. That the Wachowski brothers' previous film was the lesbian thriller *Bound*, and that Andy Wachowski has been reported to be a cross-dressing sadomasochist, photographed with a dominatrix at his side, also corroborates this idea.

Family trouble, fatherlessness, and gender confusion all lead to spiritual desire. Or, as G.K. Chesterton put it, "the man who knocks on the brothel door knocks for God." In all three films the protagonists are asking questions of ultimate meaning, and looking desperately for an answer. In *American Beauty*, Lester Burnham says, "I'm forty-two years old and in less than a year I'll be dead. Of course, in a way, I was dead already." In *Fight Club*, Tyler Durden says of his generation: "We are history's middle children; we've got no great war to fight, no Great Depression: our great war is a spiritual war; our great depression is our lives." Jack describes his addiction to self-help groups and then to fight club in increasingly explicitly religious terms. After group therapy he says, "Every night I died and every night I was resurrected; born again." After fight club he says, "Fight club wasn't about winning or losing, it wasn't about right or wrong. It wasn't about words. Because nothing mattered. . . ." The camera offers a close-up of spilled blood on the floor while Jack says, "Afterwards, we all felt saved." Hebrews 9:22 spells this scene's meaning out explicitly: "Without the shedding of blood, there is no forgiveness." In the novel, fight club originally takes place on early Sunday mornings only.

In *The Matrix*, Thomas Anderson ultimately chooses to overcome his Doubting Thomas nature and believe he can save Morpheus, which leads him to accept that as Neo, he is The One. For *American Beauty*'s Ricky Fitts, a dead bird, a homeless woman who has frozen to death, and a plastic bag blowing in the wind offer him access to beauty of such a kind that he feels like he can stare into the face of God. He says he is reminded "that there's this entire life behind things, telling me never to be afraid, ever. Video's a poor excuse, but it helps me remember. And I need to remember." Martin

Luther said almost this same thing five hundred years before: "We need to remember the gospel every day because we forget the gospel every day."

In addition to the larger theme of men attempting to define themselves against an overfeminized system, there are other smaller—but deeper and more detailed—connections between these three films of 1999 and *Pink Floyd The Wall* of 1982. Below are some of them. If you watch the four films back to back, you'll find others.

DOES THE MOVIE HAVE A LOVER'S TRIANGLE?

The Wall: Yes, Pink, his wife, and her peace-activist lover
The Matrix: Yes, Trinity, Neo, and Cypher
American Beauty: Yes, Lester, Angela, and Carolyn
Fight Club: Yes, Jack, Tyler, and Marla

DOES THE FILM FEATURE A BLACK FOUR-DOOR LINCOLN?

The Wall: Yes, Pink's limousine, a 1982 Lincoln Continental
The Matrix: Yes, Morpheus's 1965 Lincoln Continental
American Beauty: No, the closest we get is a 1989 Cadillac Coupe DeVille in the funeral procession scene, but Carolyn's Mercedes ML 320 SUV is a key element
Fight Club: Yes, Tyler's 1990 Lincoln Town Car in which he and Jack have "a near-life experience," which is also the same make of car that Jack investigates at the beginning of the film

IS THE FILM INCOMPLETE WITHOUT ITS HIGHLY THEMATIC SOUNDTRACK?

The Wall: Yes, Pink Floyd
The Matrix: Yes, electronica
American Beauty: Yes, classic rock and Thomas Newman's haunting score
Fight Club: Yes, The Dust Brothers' electronica

DOES THE FILM SHOW ITS PROTAGONIST TO BE METAPHORICALLY "IMPRISONED"?

The Wall: Yes, Pink is imprisoned by the Wall

The Matrix: Yes, Morpheus describes the Matrix as "a prison for your mind"

American Beauty: Yes, we see Lester Burnham imprisoned by a row of columns on his computer screen that bracket his face

Fight Club: Yes, Jack describes his apartment as "a filing cabinet for widows and young professionals"

DOES THE FILM HAVE A BATHTUB OR BATHROOM SCENE?

The Wall: Yes, the groupie who says, "Wanna take a bath?" and Pink's shaving scene

The Matrix: Yes, when Neo is "born again" out of the Matrix and into the water

American Beauty: Yes, when Lester encounters Angela in a bathtub full of roses in his fantasy sequence

Fight Club: Yes, when Tyler and Jack are discussing their fathers in the Paper Street house

DOES THE FILM HAVE AN OVERHEAD SHOT OF THE PROTAGONIST SLEEPING AND/OR IN THE FETAL POSITION?

The Wall: Yes, Pink curls up after realizing his wife isn't answering the phone

The Matrix: Yes, we first encounter Neo in a fetus-like womb of electronic gadgetry

American Beauty: Yes, when Lester is seen in his bedroom throughout the film

Fight Club: Yes, when Jack tells us, after a self-help meeting, "Babies don't sleep this well"

DOES THE FILM CONTAIN A SCENE IN WHICH THE PROTAGONIST DESTROYS PART OR ALL OF HIS LIVING SPACE?

The Wall: Yes, Pink trashes his hotel room

The Matrix: No, though Neo does do domestic damage to lobbies

American Beauty: Yes, when Lester throws the asparagus plate against a wall hung with framed art

Fight Club: Yes, when Jack blows up his entire apartment

DOES THE FILM CONTAIN "HEAD TRIPS" AND/OR FANTASY SCENES?

The Wall: Yes, the animated sequences
The Matrix: Yes, the Matrix moments all "feel" unreal until we learn otherwise
American Beauty: Yes, when Lester Burnham fantasizes about Angela
Fight Club: Yes, the entire film can be considered a "head trip"

DOES THE FILM GIVE STARRING ROLES TO NEWCOMERS?

The Wall: Yes, Bob Geldof
The Matrix: Yes, members of Morpheus's crew
American Beauty: Yes, Thora Birch, Mena Suvari, and Wes Bentley
Fight Club: Yes, Jared Leto was a newcomer to film

DOES THE FILM SHOW SCENES WITHIN IT OF A CLASSIC WAR MOVIE?

The Wall: Yes, The Dam Busters playing in Pink's hotel room
The Matrix: No
American Beauty: Yes, This is the Army playing in Col. Fitts's home
Fight Club: No

DOES THE FILM INCLUDE A SCENE IN WHICH THE PROTAGONIST MUST FACE HIS BOSS?

The Wall: Yes, if you count Pink's manager screaming at him for the drug overdose
The Matrix: Yes, when Neo's boss tells him he "has a problem with authority"
American Beauty: Yes, when Lester bribes his boss for a year's salary
Fight Club: Yes, when Jack bribes his boss for a year's salary

DOES THE FILM'S STORYLINE REQUIRE THE PROTAGONIST TO BECOME PHYSICALLY VIOLENT IN ORDER TO SUCCEED ON HIS QUEST?

The Wall: Yes, he must tear down the Wall
The Matrix: Yes, he must destroy the agents of the Matrix
American Beauty: Yes, sort of, since he must die by violence at the end
Fight Club: Yes, he has to fight

DOES THE FILM DEAL WITH SPIRITUAL DEADNESS AS ONE OF THE PROTAG-
ONIST'S MAIN ISSUES?

>*The Wall*: Yes, Pink is "comfortably numb" and must peel his face off in order to become real
>
>*The Matrix*: Yes, Thomas Anderson is in a self-induced coma
>
>*American Beauty*: Yes, Lester Burnham has never felt "this sedated" and says, "In a way, I'm dead already"
>
>*Fight Club*: Yes, Tyler awakens Jack to the reality of his autopilot zombie consumer lifestyle

TO COUNTERACT THEIR DEADNESS, DO THE FILM'S PROTAGONISTS HAVE TO
BE "BORN AGAIN"?

>*The Wall*: Yes, Pink must shave his entire body, babylike, in order to be saved
>
>*The Matrix*: Yes, Thomas Anderson must be born out of his Matrix pod, and arrive pink and hairless into Morpheus's ship, the *Nebuchadnezzar*
>
>*American Beauty*: Yes, Lester Burnham says, "I feel like I've been in a coma for twenty years. And I'm just now beginning to wake up"
>
>*Fight Club*: Yes, Jack experiences support group therapy and fight club as religious salvation: "Each night I died, and each night I was resurrected, 'born again'"

DOES THE FILM RELY HEAVILY ON THE FLASHBACK TECHNIQUE?

>*The Wall*: Yes, to Pink's former life and childhood
>
>*The Matrix*: Sort of, since the entire film can be considered a continuous series of flashbacks between the protagonist's dead life (corporate drone Thomas Anderson) and his living life (Neo, The One)
>
>*American Beauty*: Yes, to Lester's life flashing before him just as he dies
>
>*Fight Club*: Sort of, since the film can be considered a continuous series of flashbacks from the waking self (Tyler's actions) to the sleeping self (Jack's actions)

Is the film rated R?

The Wall: Yes
The Matrix: Yes
American Beauty: Yes
Fight Club: Yes

Does the film's protagonist smoke?

The Wall: Yes
The Matrix: No
American Beauty: Yes, marijuana
Fight Club: Yes

Does the film show or reference the influence of television on the protagonist?

The Wall: Yes, Pink watches, then smashes, the TV
The Matrix: Yes, Neo first understands the Matrix through a TV presentation shown to him by Morpheus, with the words DEEP SCAN on the back of the set
American Beauty: Yes, Jane and Ricky are on television simultaneous to videotaping each other, and Col. Fitts's family watches television
Fight Club: Yes, Jack refers to life in the Paper Street house with the line, "After two weeks, we didn't even miss television," and yet, at the end of the film, the members of Project Mayhem watch TV to see how much media attention their latest prank has garnered

Does the film deal explicitly in product placement or its issues?

The Wall: Yes, we see images of BMW and other corporate logos in the animated Wall sequence
The Matrix: Yes, from Nokia phones to FedEx
American Beauty: Yes, the Mercedes 430 sedan is given prominent placement, while at the same time Lester Burnham says he has been "a whore for the advertising industry for fourteen years"

Fight Club: Yes, despite being an anti-consumerist film—"the IBM Stellar Sphere, the Krispy Kreme Galaxy, Planet Starbucks"—the film nevertheless has product placement in the form of Pepsi products, Busch beer, Calvin Klein underwear, and others

DOES THE FILM HAVE AN UNREQUITED LOVE INTEREST?

The Wall: Yes, Pink never sees his wife again

The Matrix: Yes, Neo and Trinity do not consummate their relationship in the first film

American Beauty: Yes, Lester and Angela never consummate, though the original script said they did

Fight Club: No, unless you consider it a yes by virtue of the fact that Tyler and Jack never consummate

DOES THE FILM MAKE AN IMPLICIT OR EXPLICIT REFERENCE TO FASCISM?

The Wall: Yes, Pink is essentially a neo-Nazi rock star

The Matrix: Yes, the agents and the Matrix are essentially mind controllers who speak only the language of power

American Beauty: Yes, Lester Burnham refers to his job as fascist

Fight Club: Yes, fight club's members obey Tyler in a somewhat fascist manner

IS OBEDIENCE TO AUTHORITY, PROPAGANDA, AND MIND CONTROL PART OF THE FILM?

The Wall: Yes, and the protagonist tries to break free

The Matrix: Yes, and the protagonist breaks free in order to free others

American Beauty: Yes, and the protagonist tries to free himself

Fight Club: Yes, and the protagonist tries to free others after demonstrating his own freedom

DOES THE STORYLINE SEE THE PROTAGONIST DESTROY HIS WORLD ONLY TO (WITTINGLY OR UNWITTINGLY) REBUILD IT IN HIS OWN IMAGE?

The Wall: Yes, at the end, after the wall is torn down, we see small children with dump trucks playing at construction

The Matrix: Yes, at the end, Neo tells us that this is not the end but the beginning, and *The Matrix* sequels confirm this

American Beauty: Yes, sort of—Lester Burnham destroys all that he has and is, and in the character of Ricky Fitts there is an implied rebirth of wonder and beauty

Fight Club: Yes, and the film does this better than the book. The story takes us from "Planet Starbucks" to "In Tyler We Trust"; from anti-corporate propaganda—"When deep space exploration ramps up, it'll be the corporations that run everything"—and an anti-television philosophy—"After two weeks, I didn't even miss television"—to watching Project Mayhem's exploits on a TV in the Paper Street living room with both a Busch beer and a Pepsi Cola product placement shot

DOES THE PROTAGONIST WEAR BLACK, SYMBOLIZING IN SOME WAY EITHER THE STATE OR THE CHURCH?

The Wall: Yes, the neo-Nazi uniform worn by Pink and his band

The Matrix: Yes, the black leather trench coats worn by Neo and Trinity, which become full monastic collars in the sequels

American Beauty: Yes, sort of, in the character of Ricky Fitts, of whom Angela says, "Why does he dress like a Bible salesman?"

Fight Club: Yes, Project Mayhem's clothing requirement for each applicant is the new Benedictine habit of "two black shirts, two pairs of black trousers, one pair of heavy black boots, two pairs of black socks, two pairs of plain underwear, one heavy black coat"

DOES THE FILM HAVE A CRUCIAL TELEPHONE SCENE?

The Wall: Yes, when Pink tries to reach his wife on an overseas call and is hung up on

The Matrix: Yes, and the land-line phone becomes the means by which the heroes can exit the Matrix

American Beauty: Yes, it is through the phone that Jane learns her dad has a secret crush on Angela

Fight Club: Yes, it is through the phone call to Tyler Durden that we first see Jack "split" his personality, and we later see Tyler having a similar phone call to Marla Singer

DOES THE FILM HAVE A CRUCIAL GUN SCENE OR SCENES?

The Wall: Yes, the war scenes with Pink's father; Pink finds Dad's gun, places bullets on railroad tracks

The Matrix: Oh yes, "Guns: lots of guns"

American Beauty: Yes, Caroline learns from the King of Real Estate that "Nothing makes [her] feel more powerful than shooting a gun," and then she purchases one; Lester Burnham dies at the hand of one of Col. Ricky Fitts's Nazi guns

Fight Club: Yes, the story begins and ends with a gun in Jack/Tyler's mouth

MORE SPECIFICALLY, DOES THE FILM GIVE THE PROTAGONIST A GUNSHOT TO THE HEAD?

The Wall: No, though suicide is attempted

The Matrix: Many shots are fired at Neo, but none hit his head

American Beauty: Yes, Lester's head is blown off at the end

Fight Club: Yes, Tyler's head is blown off at the end

DOES THE FILM MAKE AN IMPLICIT OR EXPLICIT REFERENCE TO RONALD REAGAN?

The Wall: Yes, implicitly, as the film was released during Reagan's first term in office

The Matrix: Yes, explicitly through Cypher's "real" name of Mr. Reagan, which we learn about during his steak dinner with Agent Smith, when he agrees to betray the *Nebuchadnezzar's* crew

American Beauty: Yes, explicitly when Col. Ricky Fitts and his wife are watching television on which the 1943 movie *This is the Army*, starring a young Ronald Reagan, is playing

Fight Club: No, neither implicitly nor explicitly; the only president referenced is Abraham Lincoln

DOES THE FILM TAKE LONGER THAN THE STANDARD SCREEN TIME OF
90–120 MINUTES?

The Wall: No, 95 minutes
The Matrix: Yes, 136 minutes
American Beauty: Yes, 122 minutes
Fight Club: Yes, 139 minutes

Prisca Sondrie of L'Abri described *The Wall* as "the scream of modern man" for its movie poster, which was a thematic update of Edvard Munch's 1893 painting of anomie and existential angst against a blood-red skyline. *The Matrix*, *American Beauty*, and *Fight Club* each have their own distinct primal scream. These three films of 1999 still resonate with us today, perhaps in part because their screams have yet to be answered.

Barry Vacker teaches media, cultural, and utopian theory at Temple University, Philadelphia. He is the author of many articles and book chapters, and his recent publications include the text for Peter Granser's photography book *Signs* (2008). Vacker's recent work with experimental media includes the first three volumes of the Theory Zero book series (*Zero Conditions*, *Crashing into the Vanishing Points*, and *Starry Skies Moving Away*, 2008) and writing and directing the documentary *Space Times Square* (2007). Articles, books, and film information are available at www.barryvacker.net.

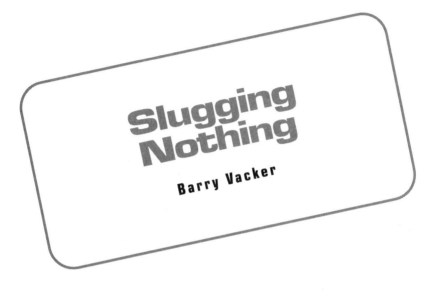

Nothingness haunts being.

—Jean-Paul Sartre

Fight the Future

"Three Minutes. This is it: Ground Zero."

So declares Tyler Durden in the first and last scenes of the film *Fight Club*. During the apocalyptic ending of the film, these words are followed by several skyscrapers collapsing to the ground, imploded by Durden's terrorist organization, Project Mayhem. In the novel *Fight Club*, only one skyscraper is detonated, yet it is described as "the world's tallest building." These words and images offered a strange anticipation of the fate of the Twin Towers in New York City, which had once been the tallest buildings in the world.* The reference to Ground Zero is instructive, for the novel and film contain many references to zeros, nothings, holes, emptinesses, which is perfectly expressed in Tyler Durden's ultimate ambition in the film—to get humanity to "go all back to zero." For Durden, toppling the skyscrapers inhabited by credit card companies would not only erase the world's plastic debt, but the zero would signal planetary chaos and destruction for modernity.

"It's Project Mayhem that's going to save the world. A cultural ice age. A prematurely induced dark age."

With these words, Tyler Durden summarizes the purposes of Project Mayhem, the terrorist network created to bring about the "destruction of civilization." By toppling skyscrapers and destroying museums, Project Mayhem seeks to create cultural "chaos" and "anarchy," and thus hasten the entropy of modernity. The aim is not merely to save the world by destroying it, but to effect a reversal, toward a cultural ice age and dark age. The destination is a retreat to Tyler Durden's premodern utopia, where a hunter-gatherer society would forage for food amidst empty skyscrapers and abandoned superhighways.

"Nothing is static. Even the *Mona Lisa* is falling apart."

Here Jack is describing the existential conditions of the universe, the conditions being embraced and enhanced by Project Mayhem. The first and second rules of fight club are famous: "You do not talk about fight club!" The first and second laws of fight club are also well known: "The Second Law of Thermodynamics." In theoretical physics, the Second Law holds that all physical systems have a tendency toward increasing entropy and disorder. Though not explicitly mentioned in *Fight Club*, the Second Law of Thermodynamics is operative throughout the book and film, with numerous descriptions and depictions of disorder, dissolution, destruction, and degeneration.

"With insomnia, nothing is real. Everything's far away. Everything's a copy of a copy of a copy."

---

*The Twin Towers were surpassed by the Sears Tower (1974) and the Petronas Towers (1998).

In the film *Fight Club*, Jack offers this lament while standing at a copy machine, on top of which is a Starbucks coffee cup. The copy machine methodically cranks out the copies, in a room full of identical workers also sipping Starbucks and making copies. Jack expresses angst over the loss of authenticity and individuality in a world of malls packed with mass-produced goods and a mass media that never sleep, running 24/7, expanding in all directions with an explosion of image and information. The real and authentic seem ever farther away, disappearing beyond the horizons of the mediated and simulated, the realms of the replica and the reproduction. The idea that "everything's far away" also echoes the fate of the Big Bang universe, expanding in all directions, with galaxies being shoved apart by expanding voids of nothingness, apparently destined to disappear beyond all horizons.

These four quotes express the existential conditions of *Fight Club*. The novel and film captured the millennial angst felt toward modernity and technology—which revealed an ever-expanding universe of vast voids with a void of meaning—and toward a *philosophy of the future* for living in such a universe. Entering the millennium, the zeros and nothings symbolize the difficulty in imagining a positive or meaningful future, or at least a future not already lived, or not already lost.

In exploring the meanings of the zeros and nothings, this essay will draw upon Jean-Paul Sartre's *Being and Nothingness*, Marshall McLuhan's *Through the Vanishing Point*, Theodore Kaczynski's *The Unabomber Manifesto*, and Brian Greene's *The Fabric of the Cosmos*. Perhaps the most radical implication for *Fight Club* will be found in Sartre's theorization of the future as a "nothingness," the nothingness of possibilities facing and shaping humanity. *Fight Club* depicts a heavyweight title fight because the philosophical bout is the fight with the future, the precise space-time parameters for *slugging nothing*.

The Zero Condition

Time is no longer counted progressively, by addition, starting from an origin—but by subtraction, starting from the end. This is what happens with rocket launches and time bombs. And that end is no longer symbolic of an endpoint of a history but the mark of a zero sum, of a potential exhaustion.

—Jean Baudrillard

To explore the significance of the nothings and zeros in *Fight Club* requires situating the novel and film within a larger pattern of events entering the millennium, where the number zero was repeatedly associated with the future. The novel and film versions of *Fight Club* were released in 1995 and 1999, respectively, precisely as culture was speeding toward the millennium. Tyler Durden sought to make humanity "go all back to zero" by effecting a "ground zero." Zero was central to the Millennium Clock, Y2K, the Millennium Dome, the Twin Towers, *Naqoyqatsi*, *The Matrix*, Coke Zero, and even the fate of the universe. The year 2000 had long been associated with the arrival of "the future," yet the recurring pattern of zeros suggested something was awry in the spirit and philosophy of that future.

The countdown to zero began at the Centre Pompidou in Paris, where the Millennium Clock ticked toward to the end of the millennium, with electronic digits showing the many millions of seconds until the arrival of 2000. Inspired by a 1980 *Le Monde* article about the end of the millennium, the Millennium Clock in Paris was the first clock to begin the countdown. Throughout 1999, the ticking surely seemed to accelerate, with the zeros increasing on the left side and eventually cascading in the final minutes and seconds to all zeros. There was climax and completion in the cascade of zeros, heralding not only the end of the millennium, but perhaps the end of the future. For Jean Baudrillard, the Millennium Clock suggested that modernity was running down, or out of time, becoming entropic in the exhaustion of all future possibilities—the project of modernity had become the "final illusion of history," for its vision of perpetual progress and industrial technology no longer existed as utopian models of the future (*The Vital Illusion*).

As the Millennium Clock was ticking toward zero, a pair of zeros appeared on the digital horizon, known as Y2K, the non-event that masked and mapped real events. Many feared that computers would not properly recognize the arrival of the year 2000, which would be recorded as "00" at 00:00:00 between December 31, 1999, and January 1, 2000. To save scarce and expensive computer space during the 1950s, calendar years were recorded by the last two numbers— "57" instead of "1957." It was thought that computers would record 2000 as "00" and conclude that the new year was 1900, thus triggering one of two possibilities—computers might make enormous financial miscalculations and wreak havoc in the world banking systems, or the computers might crash, and thus effect a technological crisis as the crash rippled through all the media and energy networks around the world. Businesses and governments enlisted programmers to "correct" the code, combining to spend an estimated $300–600 billion around the world. Though there were some minor glitches, the corrections apparently worked, for the computer networks did not crash at 00:00:00 on January 1, 2000.

As with the Cold War, the technological apocalypse was avoided with Y2K, thus masking the virtual apocalypse of mediation and simulation occurring around the world, where "reality" disappears beyond its representations in the proliferating territories of postmodern media. The new millennium finally arrived in 2001, though without "the future" as once imagined. Computers were reprogrammed for the future precisely as reality was being deprogrammed from the future, retreating behind the horizons of image and information, clones and copies, replicas and reproductions. Though computers did not crash in 2000, the future itself seems to have crashed into its own vanishing point, the very condition on display at the Millennium Dome.

The Millennium Dome was intended to be an architectural icon for celebrating the new millennium, symbolically situated on the Greenwich Peninsula, at 0° longitude on the prime meridian, which functions as the beginning and end point in the standardization of world time. Made from a translucent glass-fiber fabric, the Millennium Dome is the largest dome in the world, spanning three hundred and twenty meters and supported by twelve towering masts protruding through the roof. Inside the Millennium Dome was the Millennium Experience, a series of Zones designed to be educational and entertaining, each dedicated to some aspect of the human condition at the millennium. Functioning like a synthesis of world's fair and theme park, the Millennium Dome and Millennium Experience opened on December 31, 1999, and closed on December 31, 2000. Promotional literature described the Zones as "windows to the future," with the Millennium Dome being "the most forward-looking place in the world to celebrate the year 2000 and our voyage into the next thousand years."

The most popular Zone was the Body, where visitors walked inside a giant human body (the size of the Statue of Liberty) that featured a pumping heart, brain activities, and other bodily functions. The Mind depicted the functions and neural networks of the brain. The Home Planet offered a multimedia presentation about nature around the world, with an exterior made of TV screens showing various images of nature. The Living Island explored the human impact on the environment, effected through a simulation of a British seaside port, complete with a beach and the sea. Other Zones included Work, Play, Money, Faith, Learning, and Journey (transportation), each experienced much like a theme park attraction.

What can be made of this future displayed at 0°? The Planet was a multimedia experience, and the Living Island simulated ecology. Looking much like the Internet, the networks of the Mind were mapped and the "windows to the future" opened on a Disney-like vision of tomorrow. After the Millennium Experience closed, the exhibits and everything inside were dismantled and sold via an auction—a fire sale of "the future." By the end of 2001, the Millennium Dome was an empty cavern, containing nothing more than dust and debris. In less than a year, the Millennium Dome had gone from a world full of the future to a world of technological nothingness.

If the Millennium Dome was about the future, then it seems we have entered a disposable future, or an empty future, or perhaps a future dead on arrival. Perhaps this future is suggested by the fate of the Body, for which there were no bidders, apparently because the giant human form was too unwieldy or just plain useless. After being dismembered, the Body was buried in a nearby hole. The only full-time resident of the Dome is already dead, the Body now decaying in its graveyard. The Body entered the future at 0° and was buried shortly after at 0°, at the beginning and end of world time.

Dedicated to celebrating the "future" of the space and information ages, the 1964 New York World's Fair included the debut of the Twin Towers, which were featured in a model of New York City. Originally conceived as a vertical world's fair, the Twin Towers were the first skyscrapers wired for global telecommunications. The World Trade Center was completed in 1973, and when Tower 2 was finished, it became the mirror of Tower 1, thus making the monoliths into icons for the copy, the clone, the replay of the event that had already occurred, the arrival at a destination that already had been reached. The Twin Towers were like binary digits, the 1s turned on, towering monoliths waiting for the countdown to (ground) zero. The people killed in the collapse of the Twin Towers were disintegrated and buried at a zero, not unlike the Body dismembered and buried at 0°L near the Millennium Dome. Conceived like world's fairs to celebrate the future, the Millennium Dome and the Twin Towers both met unexpected fates—burials at two zeros, two funerals for a new future, now apparently dead on arrival.

The events at Ground Zero in New York City were anticipated in Las Vegas, at the hotel New York–New York. Opened in 1997, New York–New York embraced the metaphysics of the clone and the copy, for the hotel is a giant simulation of various icons in New York City—a half-size Statue of Liberty, forty-seven-story Empire State Building, Chrysler Building, Seagram Building, Grand Central Station, three-hundred-foot-long Brooklyn Bridge, and many others. Within New York–New York, tourists can dine in Greenwich Village or stroll along Times Square and Broadway. However, visitors have never been able to visit the World Trade Center, for the Twin Towers were not included in the skyline of New York–New York. Like a map prophesying the *absence* of territories, the future of New York City was presaged in the Xerox of New York–New York. While the Twin Towers disappeared in Vegas before Manhattan, skyscrapers and the Superdome towered above swamps in flooded New Orleans, the site for yet another Ground Zero in the American metropolis, and perhaps a test run for the coastal effects of global warming.

The zero condition was extended to the universe in *Naqoyqatsi* (2002) by Godfrey Reggio and The Matrix trilogy (1999, 2003) by the Wachowski brothers. In the first film, after the word "NAQOYQATSI" is shown at the beginning, a burst of stars accelerates toward us, expanding in all directions. A zero emerges from around the four sides of the screen and then recedes into the vanishing point, while the stars accelerate ever faster, becoming a blur of white light. The zero reemerges from behind the expanding stars, accompanied by a horizontal stream of 1s and 0s that dissolve into exploding stars. Similar imagery was depicted in The Matrix trilogy, especially in the opening scenes of all three films. *Naqoyqatsi* and The Matrix vividly theorize the existential conditions of the information age, an ever-accelerating journey into virtuality, into the vanishing point, the zero, nothingness.

This journey into end-of-the-millennium nothingness parallels some of the insights offered by cutting-edge cosmological theory, especially the superstring theory. Superstring theory posits that the smallest constituents of the universe are not particles of matter but loops of energy, in the form of submicroscopic strings, which are linked together like a complex web or membrane. The smallest of these loops are called "zero-branes," and, like strings on a guitar, the loops of energy vibrate to generate the matter of the universe. Though not yet empirically verified, the equations suggest the strings make up a sprawling cosmic fabric upon which exists the matter of the universe. Since the Big Bang, the universe has been expanding in all directions, with the galaxies hurtling away from each other with increasing velocity. Propelling the universe apart are the expanding voids in between the galaxies. Almost completely empty, these voids are like intergalactic nothingnesses, always expanding, apparently spreading the universe toward a final state of zero density and "zero curvature," or toward a flat universe that has disappeared beyond all horizons. Physicist Brian Greene likens the shape of the universe to a flat-screen TV and a hologram on a plastic card, where reality exists on a thin surface illuminated to reveal "the holographic illusions of daily life." If the Second Law of Thermodynamics and superstring theory are correct, then the ultimate trajectory of the universe is from infinite energy and density toward zero energy and zero density.

Offering the promise of zero energy and zero density, Coke Zero may be the ultimate cosmic soft drink. Introduced in 2005, Coke Zero's "zero formula" contains zero calories, zero carbohydrates, zero sugar, zero protein—apparently meaning that the drink offers nothing to increase energy and nothing to increase the density of body fat, though apparently it still contains caffeine for a quick hit. From Coke to Diet Coke to Coke Zero, the trajectory of the original Coca-Cola is to disappear, to have its flavor simulated and function emptied, to reach its vanishing point on the horizons of the global marketplace. Like a copy of a copy of a copy, Coke Zero is the soft drink simulacrum, the virtual beverage. Once promoted as "the real thing," Coca-Cola has cloned a near nothing, marketed as nothing, a zero, in Coke Zero.

On the five-year anniversary of September 11th, the *New York Times* published a special section called "Broken Ground: The Hole in the City's Heart." On the first page was a circular photograph of New York City with Ground Zero at the center of the image and the rest of the city and world warping away toward the vanishing points. Wittingly or unwittingly, the *New York Times* depicted New York City as a zero, for what else is a circle with a hole in it—especially a hole called Ground Zero—but the site and symbol for both nothingness and singularity? In the book and film *An Inconvenient Truth*, Al Gore argues that humanity faces the moment of singularity for confronting global warming, which can only be reversed by a "zero-carbon" tomorrow.

In 2007, the zero appeared on a global scale, hovering above the clouds against a blue sky. On either side of the zero was a capitol *S*, spelling out "SOS," the famed letters signaling distress or emergency. The zero was the centerpiece of the logo for Live Earth, the global "concerts for a climate in crisis." Upon arriving at the Live Earth Web site, visitors viewed each *S* disappearing behind the *O*, the center of which was black. Beside the *O* were the words "Live Earth" and if one scrolled over the two words, "Live Earth" disappeared against the black background, leaving only the *O*, the circle that became a zero, signaling countdown to the ecological apocalypse or blastoff for a zero-carbon tomorrow.

In the television documentary *Aftermath: Population Zero* (2008), special effects depicted what would happen on Earth if humans instantly vanished from the planet. Within seconds, cars are crashing; within minutes, planes are dropping from the sky. Within hours, the unattended power grid is shutting down and the entire planet is dark at night. Within ten years, roads are cracked and being covered with weeds; nature is beginning to green the cities. Within thirty years, satellites are crashing to Earth, pulled down by gravity. Within two hundred years, many skyscrapers and bridges begin to collapse because of rust and decay. Within one thousand years, the Eiffel Tower and Statue of Liberty collapse, falling beneath the green canopy, the urban rainforest of Tyler Durden, to be followed by a global ice age. Within twenty-five thousand to one hundred thousand years, the next ice age will send glaciers grinding across the collapsed cities and erasing any last remnants of the human species; on Earth, all traces of humanity have reached the vanishing point, the zero condition.

The fascination with zeros and nothingness reached art galleries and the ivory towers. There were two art exhibits on nothingness— "Nothing" opened in 2001 at the Northern Gallery for Contemporary Art in Sunderland, UK, before continuing at galleries in Lithuania and Sweden; "The Big Nothing" exhibit was held during 2004 at the Institute for Contemporary Art, located on the University of Pennsylvania campus in Philadelphia. Other than images of zeros and holes, the works in these exhibits scarcely provided interesting or insightful visualizations of nothingness, perhaps unintentionally suggesting the contemporary art world's own intellectual emptiness qua nothingness. However, some essays in the companion book for "Nothing" offered insights into the connections between nothingness in art and science, and suggested a few symbolic connections between "nothing, apocalypse, and utopia," the themes implicit in the zero conditions. More comprehensive scientific accounts appeared in three books published about the science of nothingness and three books about the history and science of zero—

Robert Kaplan's *The Nothing That Is: A Natural History of Zero* (1999), Charles Seife's *Zero: The Biography of a Dangerous Idea* (2000), and Chet Raymo's *Walking Zero: Discovering Cosmic Space and Time Along the PRIME MERIDIAN* (2006).The post–September 11th cultural critique of Paul Virilio was entitled *Ground Zero*.

So, what do these zeros signify? As first suggested by the Millennium Clock, the zeros suggest that modernity is running down, becoming entropic in its exhaustion as a model of the future. The year 2000 once symbolized the arrival of "the future," yet as humanity approached the millennium, there seemed to be a declining confidence in the future, even a fear of the future. Born in an era of glowing technological confidence, the twentieth century ended in an age of growing technological skepticism, caused by fears of various apocalypses, from nuclear war to global warming to worldwide computer crashes. For many, it seemed difficult to imagine an optimistic technological future. The zeros suggest not only the entropy of modernity, but also the emergence of postmodernity, the future of mass-mediation and mass-reproductions, the future of copies, clones, replicas, reproductions, simulations, nothings, and zeros. Modernity and postmodernity: these are the two futures fought in *Fight Club*. The hipster terrorists in *Fight Club* were confronting the zero condition.

Project Mayhem vs. Project Modernity

> *The Parker-Morris building will go over, all one hundred and ninety-one floors, slow as a tree falling in the forest.*
>
> —Jack

While there are many themes in *Fight Club*, the trajectory of the plot follows the emergence of a violent rebellion against the modern world, centered around brutal fistfights among gangs of men in an underground network of fight clubs. Project Mayhem and the fight clubs are organized by an alienated corporate drone named Jack, under the inspiration of his alter ego, Tyler Durden, who takes the physical form of a Luddite hipster terrorist, clad in urban grunge anti-fashion fashions. Like any bureaucratic organization, Project Mayhem had its various divisions and committees, which included the Bureaucracy of Anarchy, Organized Chaos, the Misinformation Committee, the Arson Committee, and the Assault Committee. From the fistfights, Project Mayhem soon expanded its scope and ambition to include anything from detonating computers to destroying sculptures to demolishing skyscrapers. Over the course of the novel and film, it becomes apparent that Tyler Durden is an urban Unabomber, not theorizing in the forest and mail-bombing scientists, but taking action in the metropolis and bombing skyscrapers, to get us to "go all back to zero."

So, how does *Fight Club* fit within the pattern of zeros? And how does this reflect a crisis in philosophies of the future?

The most explicit parallel is the toppling of skyscrapers in New York City. Like the New York–New York hotel, Tyler Durden offered the apocalyptic prophesy of "Ground Zero" before events of September 11th in New York City. In the book *Fight Club*, the toppled skyscraper was the fictional Parker-Morris tower, described as "the world's tallest building," which was true of the World Trade Center upon its completion in 1973. In the final scene of the film *Fight Club*, several skyscrapers are toppled, with the monoliths collapsing in a manner strikingly similar to the collapse of the Twin Towers two years later. Project Mayhem waged war on modernity and globalization, not unlike the Unabomber, the professor-turned-terrorist who mail-bombed scientists, and the terrorists who piloted planes into the Twin Towers. Project Mayhem was an army of urban Unabombers, though operating with much more powerful explosives than mere mail bombs.

The Millennium Clock thus seems prophetic, for countdowns are used when launching rockets and detonating bombs. The book *Fight Club* begins with a similar countdown—"ten minutes," "nine minutes," "eight minutes" and eventually down to "three minutes." Then follows the book's Ground Zero, the detonation of the bombs and the toppling of the skyscraper. Ground Zero was the zero to begin the cultural apocalypse. And Y2K was imagined to be the zeros that would trigger the technological apocalypse, precisely at the end of the century and millennium. At Ground Zero, Project Mayhem hoped to effect a Y2K, what many in 1999 feared would be a technological and cultural apocalypse in 2000.

However, Y2K was the non-apocalypse that masked the virtual apocalypse, for advancing technology has not caused the end of the world, but has hastened the end of "the real" in the cultural worlds. In the film *Fight Club*, Jack references this condition while making copies at a machine: "With insomnia, nothing is real. Everything's far away. Everything's a copy of a copy of a copy." In Jack's IKEA-furnished apartment, the furniture was all mass-produced derivatives of derivatives of modernism, seemingly made more real and authentic with the designer names—Johanneshov armchair, Rislampa/Har paper lamps, Alle cutlery, Vild hall clock, Steg nesting tables, and so on. The age of mass production is being overtaken by the age of mass customization and mass reproduction, where simulation is becoming the dominant operating principle.

If modernity sought to produce "the best of all possible worlds," then postmodernity seeks less to produce than to *re*produce, to recreate and replicate all previous worlds. The real is that which can be reproduced, where the real and fictional converge in models of simulation. These are the conditions symbolized by Las Vegas, perfected in the real virtualities of New York–New York and Paris, Las Vegas. Perhaps this is the destiny of the information age, the future of replication and reproduction, cloning and copying. Thus it is no surprise that the new millennium was celebrated in the Millennium Dome, with its Zones offering simulations—simulations not only of the future, but simulations *as* the future. As a first home for the millennium, the Millennium Dome soon stood empty and in disrepair, while the Body was rendered useless and buried in a hole at 0°L— the ground zero for the future. As one of Tyler Durden's "space monkeys" explains to another space monkey: "You are the same decaying organic matter as everyone else, and we are all part of the same compost pile."

The fight clubs are held in abandoned basements and empty parking garages, featuring brutal fistfights and violent assaults on the body. The fights end when one man can no longer continue, symbolically dying in a hole. As Jack declares in the film *Fight Club*: "On a long enough time line, the survival rate for everyone drops to zero." This is the condition symbolized by the fights, for everyone eventually loses a fight at fight club, just as everyone eventually dies and has no more future. Eventually, we all become part of the past. Fight club sought to hasten our arrival.

In another sense, the fights symbolized the reality we all inhabit, the ultimate reality: our bodies. In an age of fast food, fat people, and fad diets, all existing in a metrosexual media landscape of six-pack abs, hair transplants, and Viagra, there is ever more cultural pressure to improve the male body, to lose weight, grow hair, get ripped, and stay hard—just like Tyler Durden (Brad Pitt) in the film version of *Fight Club*. Yet, ultimately, the fights weren't about improved toughness, living more fully, or being more authentic. They were brutal battles aimed at the destruction of reality, of self, of improvement, of the future. "Self-improvement is masturbation; now self-destruction, that's improvement," says Tyler, in response to Jack's comment about a Calvin Klein underwear ad and guys in gyms trying to look like guys in ads. In the end, the fights are about burying the cultural body and resurrecting the brainless body, the vessels of the unthinking true believer, the follower, the conformist, the drone, the space monkey. In *Fight Club*, the narcissist metrosexuals are countered by the conformist space monkeys, consumers of Calvin Klein are countered by clones of Tyler Durden. Like the latest urban hipsters, all the "space monkeys" dressed in black—"two black shirts, two black pants." One space monkey reads from Tyler's manifesto to an assembly of space monkeys: "Our culture has made us all the same. No one is truly white or black or rich, anymore. We all want the same. Individually, we are nothing."

Fight Club is the latest in a long line of attempts to resist modern mass society, or consumer society, and the desire for authenticity and autonomy. Beginning with the beatniks of the 1950s, there have been continual efforts to resist mass culture and consumer society, to create a revolutionary counterculture, including hippies and leftists, punks and fundamentalists, goths and gangstas, Luddites and anti-globalization protestors, and so on. The new struggle is less a war on poverty than it is a war on homogeneity, seeking authenticity in a culture of mass production, seeking identity in a culture of mass mediation, seeking roots in a culture of rapid acceleration. While all these countercultural groups claim to have escaped the mass mind, their efforts to resist or revolt seem to have provided more markets for capitalism, be it corporate or entrepreneurial capitalism, apparently ever ready to create and manufacture the lifestyles of the proliferating countercultures. To satisfy these new markets of "resistance," capitalism has evolved from mass production to mass customization to mass simulation, cloning and copying all possible lifestyles for experiential consumption. With communism imploded and capitalism imperial, there are no competing economic systems on the world stage, only competing lifestyles within a global village. Fueled by counterfeit individualism and simulated authenticity, rebellion is now a consumer lifestyle, and revolution is a market niche—the Coke Zero of revolution.

As it is in *Fight Club*, so it is around the world. Fundamentalists and terrorists of all stripes—from theological to ecological to ideological—are waging wars with the perceived ills of the modern project, especially environmental harm and the imperatives of secularism and consumerism, which are spread through technological and cultural globalization. By the end of the century, modernity was charged with delivering too much material abundance, filling up the cultural world with machines and metropolises, skyscrapers and suburbs, cars and computers, and so on. Modern production filled the cultural universe with material things, but modern science revealed a cosmic universe of vast voids and no self-evident meaning. Precisely as science and technology reveal a complex and expanding universe, fundamentalists and terrorists seek a return to technological simplicity and spiritual purity in a shrinking cultural world, sort of like the Big Bang being countered by the Big Crunch. At a deeper level, Project Mayhem and fight club were not merely battling modernity, but were waging war against one of the key space-time parameters of the modern project—the idea of an optimistic and enlightened future. Tyler Durden and the space monkeys were fighting the future, struggling to hasten the end of the future, to effect a reversal of the trajectory of tomorrow, symbolized by getting humanity to "go all back to zero."

From Nothingness to Culture to Detonating IKEA

> *Nothingness lies coiled in the heart of being.*
> —Jean-Paul Sartre

If *Fight Club* depicts wars with modernity and postmodernity, a fight with two futures, then exactly how does that equate with "slugging nothing"?

To explore this question, we should turn to Jean-Paul Sartre and the existential ontology theorized in *Being and Nothingness*. Sartre believed that all human culture mediates between two realms—existence and consciousness. Simply put, culture emerges from the inherent need for humanity to mediate between existence and consciousness, between being and nothingness, to create a culture for an imagined future, the future that shapes the present.

Sartre viewed existence as everything, the entirety of the universe, seeing consciousness as part of existence and so naturally oriented to apprehending that existential universe. Existence is "being-in-itself," the universe as it is, always completely full and utterly indifferent to the fate of humanity. As with all living things, consciousness is "being-for-itself," always in a state of lack, forever seeking the fullness and completeness that motivate all thought and action. To have a lack or be incomplete is to not have something, or to have a nothing that needs to be filled with something. For Sartre, a lack or incompleteness is a *nothingness* that exists in contrast to *being*. If humans were completely full of being and without some kind of nothingness, then there would be no reason to engage in any thought or action directed toward the future. In sum, nothingness exists and humans strive to improve or complete ourselves by filling nothingness with being. Just as zero is a real number, nothingness is a real thing.

This empirical nothingness is the ground for two other nothingnesses central to *Fight Club*—the nothingness of consciousness and the nothingness of the future.

Sartre theorized consciousness as the nothingness through which we experience all being, the center for the subjective experience of existence and the things of the empirical world. To be aware of any empirical thing, consciousness must not be that thing, much like seeing is separate from what is seen. Since all things are potential objects of consciousness, consciousness must be a non-thing, or a nothingness. In effect, Sartre saw consciousness functioning much like a flashlight scanning a dark room—a beam of light illuminating existence. Consciousness illuminates existence as it is, as being-in-itself. Since consciousness is being-for-itself, it can also illuminate existence as it is not, but could be, revealing nothingnesses to be filled.

Nothingness exists—in both existence and consciousness—and such nothingness is the existential discontinuity in a deterministic universe, the starting point for all human freedom and cultural possibility, collectively and individually, from past to present to future. Thus it is no surprise that the film *Fight Club* opens with a journey through the neural networks of Jack's brain, the seat for consciousness, the site for cognitive nothingness and all cultural possibility. From the neural networks, the journey exits the brain between Jack's eyebrows, where he stares down the barrel of a gun, stuck in his mouth by Tyler Durden. From the nothingness of all possibility, Jack faced his two alternatives—blow out his brains or blow up the world.

In its evolutionary and existential incompleteness, humanity is always striving for fullness and completeness, always seeking to fill nothingness with being. Humanity will always confront a double-sided existence, the world as it is and as it could be, a Möbius existence of being and nothingness. Only through experiencing existence can human consciousness begin to fill the nothingnesses of consciousness with the ideas, knowledge, philosophies, and the systems of thought that produce culture. To fill the nothingnesses of existence and consciousness, humans can either adapt to existence or adapt existence to themselves. The adaptation to existence has occurred through biological evolution across the eons, while the adaptation of existence to consciousness has occurred through cultural evolution across the millennia, from the past to the present to the future, from premodern to modern to postmodern societies, from hunter-gatherer to agrarian to industrial to information societies. These societies emerged from the identification of existence as it is not (a nothingness) and as it could be (a possibility), which produced what it is (being, reality).

Humanity rarely experiences existence directly, in sheer and unmitigated forms. Virtually all humans spend their entire lives inhabiting some form of technological mode of existence, from premodern (agrarian) to modern (industrial) to postmodern (information, media). Seeking to fill nothingnesses, these societies emerged from the evolving technology deployed in the drive toward completeness, in the desire to overcome material and informational scarcities in culture and consciousness. The ambition of agrarian culture was to fill a lack—to overcome the scarcity of food in society through the plow and improved methods of farming. The ambition of mass production was also to fill a lack—to overcome material scarcity, to use factories to fill nothingnesses with an abundance of goods. A similar ambition exists with mass media, where the original goal was to fill a lack in consciousness, to use media technologies to fill a nothingness in knowledge with information and representations of the world. Filling these nothingnesses was at the heart of modernity and the enlightenment—it represented progress into a better future. In fact, the very nature of progress was to fill the future!

Modernity and mass production offered a domestic fullness and completeness that Jack explicitly rejected in *Fight Club*. To blow up the world required an older form of consciousness, a consciousness destined to be emptied of scientific and technological knowledge, the intellectual devolution from modern to premodern. With the rise of industrial culture, it was believed that mass-produced abundance would eliminate scarcity to satisfy the needs and wants of the masses, thus liberating them from centuries of poverty and domestic squalor. Industrialization was able to fill the lives of the masses with a quantity of goods previously unimaginable, yet it was in response to mass production that the desire for authenticity and individuality appeared as a cultural force. The system of mass production led to the culture of mass consumption, with homes filled and fashioned with designer goods and designer clothing, illustrating the transition from use-value to symbolic-value and status-value.

The furniture in Jack's IKEA-filled apartment was mass-produced, yet was seemingly customized to his personal needs via a simulated authenticity, as implied by the many designer items. Though Jack's apartment was *filled*, it was empty of meaning to him. Feeling trapped in a life too full of goods, Jack sought liberation from the mass-produced abundance, from the artworks and material goods of the IKEA lifestyle—"Then you're trapped in your lovely nest and the things you used to own, now they own you." Jack begged Tyler for deliverance:

> Deliver me from Swedish furniture.
> Deliver me from clever art. . . .
> May I never be complete.
> May I never be content.
> May I never be perfect.
> Deliver me, Tyler, from being perfect and complete.

The deliverance is realized when the apartment and the IKEA goods are detonated—the apartment went from fullness to emptiness, from being to nothingness. In conditions of complete fullness, no action is possible, which is why Tyler had to detonate the apartment, to create Jack's nothingness that makes possible truly free actions. The destruction of consumer fullness is a microcosm of Project Mayhem's overall plan, whereupon the mass-produced fullness of culture must be destroyed to create the nothingnesses from which an old freedom emerges, a savage freedom bent upon cultural destruction. As Tyler explains: "It's only after you've lost everything that you're free to do anything."

Jack's detonation of the IKEA lifestyle suggests more than a battle against consumer society, for the goods destroyed were distant derivatives of designs born of modernity. After all, that is the specialty of IKEA, a derivative modernism, a modernism made cozy and comfy. For furniture consumers, the simulacra of IKEA is the closest they will ever get to sitting in designs by the real modernists, such as Le Corbusier, Mies van der Rohe, Frank Lloyd Wright, or Buckminster Fuller. The conceptual understanding of *modern* furniture and architectural design is largely absent in the cities around the world, leaving millions of people unable to distinguish between intellectual appreciation for modernism and the simulation of taste that fuels shallow and trendy consumerism—the very intellectual condition facing Jack. In this domestic void, we find chains like IKEA offering low-cost simulacra, which look cheap and feel spiritually empty— like copies of derivatives of knock-offs of originals. The overwhelming majority of consumers have rejected domestic modernism anyway, opting for the mass-produced crafts and simulated authenticity of Home Depot or the mass-produced styles of Martha Stewart, where devolutionary traditionalism is masked as domestic perfectionism. IKEA, Home Depot, and Martha Stewart are the three design concepts that fill the American home, and only one is a distant derivative of modernism, the one detonated in *Fight Club*.

That Jack detonates IKEA is instructive, for no matter how derivative, IKEA is the retail chain most closely associated with mass-produced modernism, the design associated with progress and the future. While Jack's IKEA goods were spread all over the street below, there is one description that is most suggestive: "My Audi was still parked in the lot, but a Dakapo halogen torchiere was speared through the windshield." With a halogen-tipped spear in its windshield, mechanized modernity faced the non-illuminated dark age, existing no longer as a vision of the future. And, since modernism was always about the future, Jack was detonating the future, creating a nothingness to confront nothingness.

From Nothingness to the Future to Destroying Skyscrapers

The Future is the continual possibilization of all possibles.
—Jean-Paul Sartre

Sartre theorized the future as another nothingness, a nothingness that shapes the past and present. Humans are always negotiating between existence and consciousness, between being and nothing-ness, through actions based on plans for the future. The future is the ultimate target for slugging nothing in *Fight Club*.

Since the future has not happened yet, it is an existential noth-ingness of possibilities facing and *shaping* humanity. The future is made present and made real through the plans produced by human consciousness, the nothingness that seeks to fill the being of the future. Of course, these plans have intended and unintended conse-quences, such as nuclear power (intended) and nuclear meltdowns (unintended) or fossil fuels producing energy (intended) and fossil fuel carbons producing global warming (unintended). In any event, when we develop a plan for the future, it functions to shape our present actions, which are predicated on the possible future we have imagined. When the present happens, it immediately becomes the past, which is being-in-itself, precisely because it is full and com-plete and cannot be changed. The present world is always situated upon two trajectories, at once retreating into the past and on a per-petual flight toward the future.

The theory of the future as a nothingness applies to human actions, collectively and individually, for the cultural worlds emerg-ing from our choices and actions are predicated on a possible future we have imagined. That this essay exists now, in the present, was predicated on the fact of its non-existence, a nothingness in the future that I filled with the ideas and words you are now reading. The existence of my Macintosh laptop is predicated on it first having non-existence, a nothingness in the future filled by the technologists and designers at Apple. Similarly, the existence of agrarian, industrial, and information societies were predicated on their non-existence, as nothingnesses of the future imagined as possible. Collectively and individually, we transcend ourselves in imagining the future, in planning ahead, and projecting ourselves into the plan, into our possibilities.

At any given moment, humans are astride a nothingness, a dis-continuity between past and future, yesterday and tomorrow. Within finite existence, the nothingness of consciousness provides "infinite" possibilities (*Being and Nothingness*). The nothingnesses in existence, consciousness, and the future provide the "Big Bang" for humanity and culture, making possible an ever-expanding universe of futures.

Sartre believed that humans are always negotiating these existential conditions based on visions of the future, expressed in the desire for "a mode of being" (*Existentialism and Human Emotions*). In its many forms, culture mediates between humans and existence to provide a mode of being, a shared mode of existence for society. A central component of culture is technology, which is deployed to fill nothingnesses in creating a mode of existence. Through technology, humans long ago began transforming the world as it is into the world as it could be, adapting the world to us in creating a new world—the world of the future. From plow to printing press, factory to electricity, car to computer, there is hardly any aspect of human existence that has not been reordered through technology, with an eye toward the future, toward how the world could be, toward a new and improved mode of existence. Modernity was always a futurist project, and the twentieth century was that most modern of centuries, when it was believed that science and technology would deliver the future, the future as a mode of existence—the world of tomorrow.

Humans have surrounded themselves with a technological mode of existence, a cultural world filled with industrial and information technologies. This mode of existence includes the electrified metropolises of towering skyscrapers and sprawling suburbs, the mechanized mobility of automobiles and airplanes, the mass media of televisions and computers, the mass-produced abundance of shopping centers and strip malls, homes and residences brimming with goods reflecting the desires and dreams of the masses. The world of tomorrow made real, the future made present, this was the technological mode of existence that Project Mayhem sought to destroy in *Fight Club*—"Fight club is tomorrow, and I'm not going to miss fight club."

Ironically, the modern world is entropic, even in its expansion, for it is being eroded by the emerging technologies born of industrial culture. At its zenith in the 1950s, the industrial age gave birth to two other technological ages—the space age and the information age. The mechanized world may have extended beyond all cultural horizons, disappearing beyond the vanishing points of modernity, but it has crashed into a new set of vanishing points, the mediated world of postmodernity and the expanding universe of the Big Bang.

Born of electronic media, especially television and the computer, the information age signaled the emergence of a new mode of existence, a new global culture centered around the production and exchange of image and information, symbol and simulation—circulating in vast networks of mediated realities, each refracting and reliant upon the others as they replicate in a culture of endless symbolic consumption and simulated individuality. Always on, running 24/7, these are the networked territories of the global village, electronic territories generated by media technologies that span the cultural world as they envelop and reproduce the physical world. If the electronic media are deployed to map the surrounding world, then it seems the maps have so proliferated they are supplanting and generating the territories they were supposed to represent. These are the territories of television, cinema, computers, cell phones, iPods—stored in cyberspace, circulated via the Internet, constructed in theme parks and Las Vegas.

If New York City is the modern metropolis, the skyscraper city for the mechanized world of tomorrow, then New York–New York is the postmodern metropolis, the simulation city for the mediated world of tomorrow. Both have a ground zero.

The present is hurtling into the future, and Project Mayhem viewed both the present and future as negative and not worth living. To change the present one must change the future, meaning that Project Mayhem may be at war with modernity, which has shaped most of the present, but it also must battle postmodernity, which will shape most of the future. If the future (nothingness) is viewed negatively by those in the present, then the past (being-in-itself) will necessarily seem more attractive and more certain, precisely because it is full and complete. This is Tyler Durden's perspective, which made the distant past into the cultural destiny of Project Mayhem, necessary to confront a cosmos where modernity is entropic and the universe is expanding. By destroying a skyscraper, Project Mayhem surely declares war on project modernity, though it also desperately sensed the conditions of project postmodernity, the new future of expanding voids, expanding nothingnesses.

Project Mayhem vs. Project Postmodernity

Look up into the stars and you're gone.

—Jack

The existential conditions of postmodernity are revealed in two of Jack's musings about the nature of the cultural world and the cosmic universe. As discussed earlier, Jack stands at a copy machine in the film *Fight Club* and says:

> With insomnia, nothing is real. Everything's far away. Everything's a copy of a copy of a copy. When deep space exploration ramps up, it'll be the corporations that name everything: the IBM Stellar Sphere, the Microsoft Galaxy, Planet Starbucks.

Here, Jack combines concepts from the information and space ages in offering a poetic expression of the expanding media world. Simply put, we live in a mediated universe, made available by the computers of Apple and IBM, the software of Microsoft, and the global networks of the Internet and cyberspace. The solar system has been mapped by the electronic media of *Voyager* 1 and 2. The Big Bang was first theorized from images captured via telescope photography, and then verified via radio telescopes, which captured the background radiation emitted by the cosmic expansion. In this expanding universe, "everything's far away," as Jack says, and forever moving farther away.

Following Jack's intuition, perhaps we should think of humans inhabiting two expanding and overlapping worlds, one empirical and one mediated. These two worlds were produced by two Big Bangs, one natural and one technological. As predicted by Intel co-founder Gordon Moore in 1965, microprocessors have doubled in power every two years, while also shrinking in size and declining in cost. Known as "Moore's Law," this pattern has recurred for the past forty years and is expected to continue for the foreseeable future, ensuring that cyberspace will continue to expand exponentially, especially with the linking of ever-more-powerful computers via the Internet. In this global network, cyberspace is an expanding void of virtual space-time, while the electronic circuits and screens are the vanishing points for representation of space-time, all combining to produce a mediated cosmos, an electronic nothingness for representing the world.

To grasp this radical condition, we can combine the ideas of McLuhan and Sartre. McLuhan viewed all media as extensions of the senses and consciousness—simply put, spoken words are extensions of thought, print media are extensions of written words and our eyes, televisions are extensions of our eyes and ears, computers are extensions of consciousness, and so on. Extending from human consciousness around the world is a "global nervous system," a mode of electronic perception, with the cyberspace functioning as the circuited consciousness to be filled with information. McLuhan believed that the information age would reproduce information as "total environments," while also effecting a reversal of the vanishing point in the history of Western representation (*Through the Vanishing Point*).

For McLuhan, natural light and electric light were pure information, with light *shining on* the objects of the world, on the pages of the book, on the screens of cinema. In contrast, television and computers deploy light *shining through* the electronic screens, shining upon our faces, in effect making our eyes the screen. Rather than provide a vanishing point extending from the eye to the distant horizon, television and computers collapse space and time in the instant retrieval of information, now shining through the screens, and thus reversing the vanishing point of representation. For McLuhan, the effect is a media implosion of the world on the screens and in the circuits of cyberspace, an implosion destined to accelerate all events.

If we understand consciousness as a nothingness (Sartre) and the media as extensions of consciousness (McLuhan), then we can see how the media function as electronic nothingnesses. Mediating between existence and consciousness is yet another consciousness, an electronic mode of perception, extending around the world to become a new mode of existence, a total media environment. In the postmodern zero condition, modernity is entropic, and we have crashed into the new future of electronic screens, into the vanishing points, not situated upon the distant horizons, but rather in the circuits of cyberspace and consciousnesses, both realms of nothingness for representing being.

These are the mediated conditions suggested by the zero universes in *Naqoyqatsi* and The Matrix trilogy, both of which mapped the Big Bang of the universe within the Big Bang of the media cosmos. To confront the future of an expanding nothingness, Project Mayhem drills holes in the monitors of personal computers, fills them with liquid explosives, and detonates the computers. If, as McLuhan suggested, information is light, the light that shines through computer screens, then the light must be stopped with a premature "dark age," the very ambition of Project Mayhem.

In the war with project modernity, Jack detonates his IKEA-filled apartment, thus reducing it to an empty shell, a blackened nothingness. After wandering the edge of the exploded hole in the side of the building, fifteen stories up, Jack offers the following thoughts:

> Go to the edge of the floor, fifteen stories above the parking lot, and look at the city lights and stars, and you're gone.
>
> It's all so beyond us.
>
> Up here, in the miles of night between the stars and the Earth, I feel just like one of those space animals.
>
> Dogs.
>
> Monkeys.
>
> Men.
>
> You just do your little job. Pull a lever. Push a button. You don't really understand any of it.
>
> The world is going crazy.

Coming near the end of the book *Fight Club*, these lines illustrate that perhaps the war with project modernity has left us with an unwinnable war with postmodernity, particularly the cosmos revealed by computers and electronic media. The space age represented the high point of modernity's technological optimism, which culminated in the moon landing of 1969. Around the same time, computers and telescopes were verifying the theory of the Big Bang—the theory that the universe has been expanding for fifteen billion years, with the galaxies moving away in all directions, thrust apart by expanding voids of nothingness and apparently destined to disappear beyond all horizons, leaving a starless universe facing total entropy, the final state of the Second Law of Thermodynamics.

If the space age represents the height of technological modernity, then perhaps we are now experiencing vertigo, a condition symbolized in *Fight Club* by Seattle's Space Needle—"the Space Needle leaning at a forty-five degree angle." Rockets may have sent humans to the moon, but computers and electronic telescopes revealed a universe so vast, so unreachable, always moving away. As Jacks says: "It's all so beyond us . . . the miles of night between the stars and Earth."

For the foreseeable future, outer space will only be accessible in cyberspace (except for a few space tourists circling the Earth). Information and matter bifurcate through televisions and computers, separating image from object in space and time, leaving the object behind as the image is propelled at light speed through screens around the world. Thus the paradox of electronic media effecting an implosion of information, precisely as the universe is moving farther away in all directions. No matter how powerful our media and computers may become, the universe always will be receding from our representations of it—a flat-screen universe vanishing on the flat-screen media.

What does this mean? No one knows for sure, though cosmologists and philosophers are certain to continue debating the possibilities and developing new theories. Deep down, the Big Bang seems to support Sartre's notion of an existence utterly indifferent to humanity, a universe of mind-boggling scale, requiring that each of us take responsibility for developing the meanings for our lives. If modernity promised to fill the world with material goods, it seems that postmodernity has revealed an unfillable universe, stars amid vast empty spaces, empty of meaning, except what each of us decides. Not only is the future a nothingness, but the future will continue to exist in an ever-expanding nothingness. This is the cosmic angst of *Fight Club*.

That the rank and file members of Project Mayhem are called space monkeys is suggestive. When the term was first used by NASA in the early days of space exploration, the space monkeys were trained to push certain buttons and pull certain levers in the command module, thus allowing scientists to test the conditions for the future astronauts. Of course, the space monkeys did not understand the purpose of what they were doing, which was serving as the test subjects in the quest for outer space. Similarly, the space monkeys in *Fight Club* were the drones who were trained to execute the plans of Project Mayhem, while having no grasp of the purpose or philosophical meaning of their actions. Unlike the space monkeys of NASA, the space monkeys of Project Mayhem were not used for increasing scientific knowledge to expand the domain of technological modernity, but rather for destroying science and technology by shrinking the domains created by postmodernity. In Tyler Durden's future, living alongside real monkeys will be the space monkeys, the rulers of a real-life *Planet of the Apes*.

Future Past

This was the goal of Project Mayhem, Tyler said, the complete and right-away destruction of civilization.

—Jack

Until the industrial system has been thoroughly wrecked, the destruction of that system must be the revolutionaries' only goal.

—FC

In 1995, both the *New York Times* and the *Washington Post* published "Industrial Society and Its Future," a thirty-five-thousand-word manifesto authored by "FC"—the nom de plume for Theodore Kaczynski, the American academic-turned-terrorist also known as the Unabomber. This essay has come to be known as *The Unabomber Manifesto*, and its publication led to Kaczynski's identification and capture. In *The Unabomber Manifesto*, the Unabomber theorized the crisis of modernity and the cultural conditions supposedly caused by technological acceleration and proliferation. Perhaps Tyler Durden knew the Unabomber, for the revolution fictionalized in *Fight Club* is the same revolution theorized in *The Unabomber Manifesto*.

According to the Unabomber, mass production has been extremely adept at satisfying the "artificial" needs created in modern culture, which serve as surrogates for the "real" needs created by biological nature, such as food, clothing, shelter, and defense. For most people in most societies, industrialization has made such real needs rather easy to satisfy. However, modern culture has also created a whole slew of artificial needs that most people spend their lives trying to fulfill—from art to technology to the pursuit of wealth and luxury. Jack's apartment illustrates how a real need (shelter) is transformed into an artificial need, a home filled with IKEA items. The Unabomber argued that modernity has produced an unfulfilled and psychologically unstable society, while the technology and artifice undermine the "stable framework" found in the premodern societies.

In the future, modernity is sure to face a "desperate struggle" for survival, complete with chaotic breakdowns in the systems of nature and culture. For the Unabomber, there is but a single solution, the total annihilation of the entire industrial system. This requires the destruction of all factories, the burning of all technical books, the rejection of all but the most primitive technologies. Modern technology must be used only for the destruction of the technological system. The cultural destination was an utterly premodern culture, situated within the "wild nature," now independent of human interference and control. Humanity would inhabit a hunter-gatherer society—"peasants or herdsman or fisherman or hunters." Apparently, the thrill of the hunt and harvest will be sufficient for humans, supplanting any of the equally natural cognitive needs for art, architecture, philosophy, or any of the other artifacts of intellectual culture.

The futures imagined by Tyler Durden and the Unabomber are identical. Both men are Luddite utopians, seeking the destruction of the technological future in order to retreat to the hunter-gatherer past—the modern and postmodern followed by the premodern. Here is Tyler Durden's description of the future:

> You'll hunt elk through the damp canyon forests around the ruins of Rockefeller Center, and dig clams next to the skeleton of the Space Needle leaning at a forty-five degree angle. . . . You'll wear leather clothes that will last you the rest of your life, and you'll climb the wrist-thick kudzu vines that wrap the Sears Tower. Jack and the beanstalk, you'll climb up through the dripping forest canopy and the air will be so clean you'll see tiny figures pounding corn and laying strips of venison to dry in the empty carpool lane of an abandoned superhighway stretching eight lanes wide and August-hot for a thousand miles. This was the goal of Project Mayhem, Tyler said, the complete and utter destruction of civilization.

This is the future idealized in *Fight Club*, a premodern culture roaming amidst the ruins of the modern and postmodern worlds. The space monkeys are the noble savages of the non-information age, the next humans of the non-future, the hunter-gatherers glorified in *The Unabomber Manifesto*. In this cultural reversal, the skyscraper metropolis is replaced by the urban rain forest, the metrosexual by the space monkey, the superhighway by the walking trail, the fast food burger by the drying venison, the five-star restaurant by the campfire cookout, the joystick by the bare fist, and the Enlightenment by the fight club.

In the novel and film, *Fight Club* presents the zero condition, the Y2K future, the apocalypse after the countdown to ground zero—the Millennium Clock is succeeded by Tyler Durden's sundial, the metropolis is emptied like the Millennium Dome, the skyscraper is toppled like the Twin Towers, the expanding universe is confronted by shrinking minds, and the flat-screen cosmos is inhabited by a flat-Earth society.

By destroying civilization, Project Mayhem sought to create a nothingness for the future, a nothingness to be filled with a distant past, closer to pure nature, existence as it is, being-in-itself. Project Mayhem sought to fill the postmodern future with the premodern past, yet, in so doing, the nothingness of consciousness must be detonated, to ensure consciousness is not filled with knowledge that is modern or postmodern. In the end, *Fight Club* is still slugging nothing, blowing holes in modernity and blowing holes in minds, for at the climax of the novel, the moment when the skyscraper is detonated and Tyler pulls the trigger on the gun in Jack's mouth, this is what happened:

"And nothing. Nothing explodes."

Works Cited

Barrow, John D. *The Book of Nothing: Vacuums, Voids, and the Latest Ideas About the Origins of the Universe.* New York: Vintage Books, 2000.

Baudrillard, Jean. *The Vital Illusion.* New York: Columbia University Press, 2000.

———. *Simulacra and Simulation.* Ann Arbor: University of Michigan Press, 1994.

Cole, K.C. *The Hole in the Universe: How Scientists Peered Over the Edge of Emptiness and Found Everything.* New York: Harvest, 2001.

FC. *The Unabomber Manifesto: Industrial Society and Its Future.* Berkeley: Jolly Roger Press, 1995.

Genz, Henning. *Nothingness: The Science of Empty Space.* Cambridge, Massachusetts: Perseus, 1998.

Gere, Charles, "Nothing, Apocalypse, and Utopia" in Gussin and Carpenter, *Nothing*, 60–61.

Greene, Brian. *The Fabric of the Cosmos.* New York: Vintage Books, 2004.

Gussin, Graham, and Ele Carpenter (eds.) *Nothing*. London: August, 2001.

"The Big Nothing," The Institute for Contemporary Art. (www.icaphila.org/exhibitions/past/big_nothing.php)

Heath, Joseph, and Andrew Potter. *Nation of Rebels: Why Counterculture Became Consumer Culture*. New York: Harper Business 2004.

Kaplan, Robert, "Is It Out There?" in Gussin and Carpenter, *Nothing*, 64–76.

——. *The Nothing That Is: A Natural History of Zero*. Oxford: Oxford University Press, 1999.

McKee, Francis, "From Zero to Nothing in No Time" in Gussin and Carpenter, *Nothing*, 16–30.

McLuhan, Marshall, and Harley Parker. *Through the Vanishing Point*. New York: Harper Colophon, 1968.

Raymo, Chet. *Walking Zero: Discovering Cosmic Space and Time Along the PRIME MERIDIAN*. New York: Walker and Company, 2006.

Sartre, Jean-Paul. *Being and Nothingness*. New York: Citadel Press, 1956.

——. *Essays in Existentialism*. New York: Citadel Press, 1965.

——. *Existentialism and Human Emotions*. New York: Citadel Press, 1957.

Seife, Charles. *Zero: The Biography of a Dangerous Idea*. New York: Penguin Books, 2000.

Virilio, Paul. *Ground Zero*. London: Verso, 2002.

Dennis Widmyer is the founder and webmaster of The Cult, at www.chuckpalahniuk.net. In addition to running Chuck Palahniuk's official Web site, he is a writer and a director living in Los Angeles with a feature-length film and a documentary to his credit.

The following is based on a presentation Widmyer gave at the April 2003 Edinboro conference at the request of conference organizers, Christian McKinney and Janet Kinch. While much of this information can be found on the site already, Widmyer states that "The origin . . . the backstory . . . the true roots of this Web site were never fully fleshed out. Until now."

A Brief History of ChuckPalahniuk.net
Dennis Widmyer

One night in August of 1999 the power went out in my house. A violent rainstorm had gripped the town of Hicksville, New York, and I was suddenly thrust into a living nightmare. No computer, no TV, not even adequate candles for reading. But I did have working phones.

Fifteen minutes and a phone call later, I was sitting at a diner with my friend Amy Dalton over a plate of corned beefed hash with two eggs sunny-side up and a side order of sausage. Being fellow employees at a bookstore, we did what any self-respecting book nerds would do: We discussed authors. Amy, as always, discussed Jeff Noon. I think I may have discussed Albert Camus. The problem was neither of us had read each other's authors and so a common ground was needed.

That ground came in the form of Chuck Palahniuk. Then only the author of two books, Chuck was already a hit with my friends and me. I had purchased *Fight Club* a few years earlier, after hearing that David Fincher had optioned a screenplay called *The Fight Club*. Standing at a Borders Books and Music a couple of weeks later, holding a trade paperback in my hand, I quickly deduced that the Fincher project and the novel called *Fight Club* by some guy named Chuck Palaanee-ook (pretend like you're trying to read the front cover of the novel at this part) were, in fact, the same thing.

Ten pages into the reading of *Fight Club*, I remember feeling sort of cool. Leaning against a tree in the quad of my college campus, I had something before me that topped all the Brontës and Conrads and Millers that everyone else was reading. Here was a truly subversive novel.

Well, thirty pages into that subversive novel, and Chuck Palahniuk had quickly proven what a stranger I was to this type of fiction. Here was me, coming off a seven-year bender with the likes of Stephen King and Michael Crichton, and I was expected to enjoy a healthy dollop of Bob's bitch tits?

And so, did I bite my pillow and push on, hoping to "get" what Chuck was doing with this novel? Of course not. Instead, I passed it off to some friends. Namely my diner buddy, Amy Dalton. (pause) Then Kevin Kölsch. (pause) Then Josh Chaplinsky. To be quite honest, I think every person I knew read *Fight Club* before I did. And so finally the need to conform (and the fact that I now felt like an idiot, since they all seemed to love the book) drove me back. I returned to Bob's bitch tits . . . and this time, I stayed with it. And of course, like so many others, it soon took me over. It haunted me. It excited me. It shook me up. But most of all, it inspired me—the book, that is, not the bitch tits.

A year later, when I was working at B. Dalton bookstore, *Survivor* finally came out. I remember tearing into the Ingram shipping boxes like a reckless kid on Christmas morning. And there, in my hand, I beheld this weird, ambient, orange hardcover.

Anyway, I think you get the point. We were obsessed. Chuck's work felt *dangerous*. Like he was letting you in on some dark secret he knew so well and wanted to share. I liked *Survivor* even more than *Fight Club*. It elicited all the same emotions from me, and more. I also laughed out loud during the reading of it—something I didn't do often with the books I was forced to read in school.

So back to the diner on that stormy night. It was one week before the release of Chuck's third book, titled *Invisible Monsters*. And even better, we had discovered through the publisher's Web site that Chuck would be visiting Manhattan to do a reading. What would it be like to attend a book reading? This would be a first for us. And so we sat at the diner, talking about how we could capitalize on this situation and let the rest of the world in on our exciting little secret.

I don't know who brought up the idea of a Web site first. I do know that, at the time, I was obsessed with these silly play-by-e-mail role-playing games. I had even taken it to the next level by creating a few primitive Web sites to house all the stories and stats that went with the territory. So the idea of testing my crude Microsoft Front-Page talents on a brand new site was very exciting. But even more exciting was Chuck himself. Here was an author who could easily speak to a smart young audience . . . though because *Fight Club* the movie had not yet been released in theaters, barely anyone knew who the hell he was. At the time, I think only two to three pieces of media existed on the Web about him.

This, and the fact that I didn't recall seeing too many cool author Web sites, led us to Chuck's reading for *Invisible Monsters* in New York on September 22, 1999. Due to heavy traffic on the Long Island Expressway, we showed up late. Chuck was on the felching chapter (isn't he always?) and I remember there was a hushed smirk on everyone's faces in the audience. But who the hell was the dude behind the podium? It surely wasn't the Chuck I had envisioned. This guy resembled a tall Gordon Gekko. Dressed to the nines in a sleek blazer and slacks, Chuck even had his short hair slicked back to fit the bill even more.

After the reading ended, everyone sat in silence. A moment later, people began filing out of the small venue, but my friends and I all had this sort of dazed look on our faces. The type of look that said,

"Damn, it's even better in person!" Chuck, meanwhile, was collecting his jacket. He stood about twenty feet away as the crowd who he had awed a few minutes earlier politely exited the building. Politely ignored him.

It was one of those moments where you're not sure if you should approach the person or not. And so we exited the building along with everyone else. We stood on the cold sidewalk, feeling content enough to have just seen him read. Well, everyone was content but me. I was the idiot who kept glancing back into the main window of the venue. And there was Chuck still, chatting with a woman who I think was his publicist at W.W. Norton. If there ever was a moment to make a move, this was it.

Minutes passed and I somehow convinced myself, and the people with me, to go the hell back inside and introduce ourselves to this author who had just blown our minds. I don't know what was going through Chuck's mind when he saw me and my crowd of friends staring at him with those stupid "Wow, he's a real person!" faces. But he ended up spending ten minutes sitting with us and recounting stories about his adventures on the set of *Fight Club*. The conversation culminated with my horrible, nervous proposal for a Web site in his honor. At first I think Chuck said something like, "Are you serious?" I couldn't tell if he was flattered or confused. Either way, he gave Amy and me the go-ahead, and away we went.

The next week I redefined guerrilla tactics. I was under the gun since the movie of *Fight Club* was due out the following month. I felt like I had to get this site out before the tidal wave hit. I then realized that somebody had already beaten me to the punch. The name ChuckPalahniuk.com had already been taken. Oh well, we were to be a fan site, right? And doesn't ".net" seem more "fan-oriented"?

When the week ended, Version 1.0 of ChuckPalahniuk.net stood . . . on shaky legs. Besides a crude biography I had typed up about Chuck (gathered from the few interviews I was able to find online) the only other things we had were a few pictures, some collected reviews of his three novels, and a news page. And with the movie's release date quickly approaching, the "news" basically meant all things *Fight Club*.

Today, you go onto Google and type in the words "fight club" and you get fifteen million results. Well, in October of 1999, only two sites existed. The unofficial *Fight Club* site . . . and the official 20th Century Fox site. I quickly realized that the unofficial site needed to become our ally or else we would never be able to generate any exposure. And so I sent an e-mail to the webmaster, asking him to kindly consider our site for his links page. This same tactic served me well when I began tackling other methods of online promotion. Besides contacting every webmaster of every movie site I knew of, I did extensive searches on Yahoo! and AOL member profiles for anyone with the words "fight club," "Brad Pitt," "Edward Norton," or "Helena Bonham Carter" in their descriptions. This proved harder than it sounds. Rather then send individual e-mails to each person, I simply cheated and sent a few large group e-mails to lots of people at once. This prompted a lot of venomous hate mail in my direction.

Speaking of e-mails, there was one in particular that I must tell you about now. You see, not all my tactics were so guerrilla. I could spend days and nights promoting our site to fans and webmasters, but until Chuck himself was aware of it, I wouldn't be able to sleep at night.

The chain reaction began when I typed up a formal thank-you letter to Chuck. Here, in full, is that letter:

Dear Chuck,

First off, I apologize if this seems rude. I know you must get these all the time. Especially lately, with all the Fight Club *buzz reaching a crescendo. But this is not your usual fan mail so please, read on.*

We met a few weeks back in New York City at a place downtown called "The Drawing Center." You had just finished the reading and I was that fast-talking idiot (tall, brown hair, skinny) who cornered you and shook your hand twice. I then came back in with some friends and you were so cool that you signed all of our books. You then even took the time to chat with us for like ten mins. You basically made our month. I told everyone that story. And I also made it my purpose to get people to know your name. Even if they couldn't pronounce it right.

And so, for the next couple of weeks (I am a manager over at B. Dalton bookstore) I promoted your books up front at the register and began passing on the words of Palahniuk to all those unsuspecting readers out there. I even sold three copies of Survivor in one day once. No small feat since everyone wants Fight Club because it has that actor named Brad Pitt on the cover. Well, I even got past that. Because I ordered around seven copies of the hardcover and began to push that.

I am not telling you this so you say, "Ohh, cute. Another fan . . . only this one's a busines man." Far from it, I have an ulterior motive . . . (laughs maniacally). You might not remember, but the night we met, I mentioned that my friends and I were working on a WEB SITE for you. The first Chuck Palahniuk Web site out there. You see, we had been so disappointed and let down at the fact that the internet virtually has nothing on you. Sure, they would have small articles and Fight Club snippets and such, but nothing grand . . .

Here's where we come in. For the past three weeks now, I have been laboring my ass off (literally . . . it's sitting on the floor besides me) to create the ultimate Chuck Palahniuk Web site. Well, a few weeks ago, I was pretty much done. Now I've just been updating it with reviews, pictures, stories, facts . . . you name it, it's there. The site is called CHUCK PALAHNIUK—A Writer's Cult and it can be found at www.chuckpalahniuk.net OR the longer http://members.xoom.com/intrloper9/PalahniukMain.htm.

In the past weeks we've formed a fan base around you and people from all over the world have come out discussing your work and thanking us for our efforts. Just read the Guestbook and you'll see what I mean. We even *have spies and moles working for us who bring us info. We have someone in Portland who gets pictures and articles from the Oregonian for us. I had a fourteen-year-old kid email me telling me he had read Fight Club twice and he was unsure if, because of timing, he should still do Chapter 20 for his drama performance. I told him to go for it. Especially after hearing you read it out loud that night.*

So anyway, I once again apologize if this is an intrusion. Don't think that I hacked into your life to get your address. It was simply mailed to me by someone anonymous who had gotten it off some White Pages style list with other "P" names under it as well. Hell, it could be wrong in which case, some other Chuck Palahniuk is reading this right now laughing his ass off. If that is the case, he could make a career out of this.

Lastly, I sent this letter for two reasons:

1) To thank you for being such a cool person and taking the time to chat with us.

2) To ask you kindly to visit our Web site (www.chuckpalahniuk.net) and email me with your thoughts. Maybe even give us a review. Hell, maybe even let me give you a five questions and answers kind of thing. I have the questions all lined up. Don't worry, they don't go into Fight Club the movie. They are strictly about a man and his novels.

So check out the site or better yet, email me at EMAILREMOVED@aol.com

Thanks so much for the great words, keep 'em coming!

Dennis K. Widmyer

With the letter sent, I leaned back in my office chair and continued to work on the Web site. Our fan base was growing daily and before I knew it, we had a crowd of regulars who began sending us what would become our earliest news updates. And then, one Sunday afternoon, an e-mail came my way that changed everything:

Good Morning Dennis and Amy,

This is just a quick note to tell you I am no longer a writer. These days, I'm just a small toy that publicists push around all day. With luck, I can ditch my toy status and go back to work soon.

This morning, we're all waiting for the last weekend's "numbers" on the F/C movie. Rumored fight clubs seem to be starting around the country. Susan Faludi (author of Backlash & Stiffed) *is a fan, telling her audiences, "It was like reading my own book (Stiffed) on speed." Trent Reznor (NIN) is a fan, no surprise since I wrote most of it with* Downward Spiral *blaring in my Walkman.*

All this is happening, and now here's your amazing site. Thank you. Swamped as I am, this is a much-appreciated personal connection with someone real—the opposite of those bah-zillion flip-glib three-minute radio "interviews" or the twenty-second sound-bites on CNN. Even if we're just keyboarding back and forth, this lets me feel like a person dealing with a person. I appreciate that more than I can describe.

The night the movie opened here in Portland, I took fifty friends and they sat, keeping track of all the lines in the movie that each of them had said themselves in real life. Almost all of the book was collected from my peers, and the day I get stuck on a pedestal, disconnected from my friends, is the day I run out of ideas.

So, blah, blah, blah, send your questions. If you need proof that I'm the real C. Palahniuk, I can explain the ending to Survivor *(how he does not die).*

All My Best,
Chuck

Obviously, I was on cloud nine after that e-mail, and with a renewed determination I set out to give Chuck something he could be proud of. As the weeks and months went by, I watched as a perfect adaptation of a perfect book bombed at the box office. Yet something weird was happening. Our numbers grew and grew. It seemed like those that had seen *Fight Club* were addicted. Not only were they going back for multiple viewings, but they were quickly hopping online to devour any information they could find on this film. That always led them to our front door, and I would do my best to keep them in the house.

The chain reaction continued. The *Fight Club* DVD hit stores and became the bestselling title of the year for 20th Century Fox. Chuck's e-mails continued, and our best news updates would always end up coming straight from the horse's mouth. In this time, many *Fight Club* fan sites had sprung up, and a few Chuck Palahniuk ones, too. But our site has never been a competitive one. Rather, we flourished simply by welcoming this growing community. I even made it a point to do a feature on every new site that arose.

This community has taken on a whole new meaning for many fans, which is the reason why fans shortened our site title to simply "The Cult." Just as with Chuck's novels, fans took to our site in an almost possessive manner. It was their dark little secret—and we all know how many people have broken the first rule of *Fight Club*.

But the fans weren't the only ones obsessed. ChuckPalahniuk.net had taken me over and become my baby. I'd lie in bed at night thinking about how to improve it. I'd spend entire weeks working on the site for eighteen hours a day. On a weekend when a news update was due, you could have offered me a free ticket to Las Vegas and I'd probably pass just so I could get some work done on the site. While this work ethic never went away, it would go through the occasional up-and-down cycles. Oh yes, there were the times where I almost lost my mind. Times where I'd lose a full day's work of editing. Or times when the server moved so slow I'd have to wait two minutes just for a file to open. Or times I'd get so sick of transcribing an article or an interview that I would forget what the air outside felt like.

Yes, I'm being dramatic, but until you step into the world of the obsessed, maniacal, perfectionist webmaster . . . you cannot know. I felt like Charles Foster Kane, running a newspaper with a staff of one: me.

On a good day, we'd get a dozen or so e-mails from fans telling us how inspired they are by Chuck.

On a bad day, the server would crash and I'd spend hours e-mailing and instant-messaging the team of international players on our staff.

Today, almost a decade later, my life has changed drastically. I'm living on the other side of the country. I'm thirty. And the Internet has changed drastically, too. But Chuck Palahniuk continues to become a literary icon. His fan base grows at a staggering rate. I go to clothing stores and see his books displayed. I see him on late-night television being interviewed by Conan O'Brien and in the pages of *Rolling Stone* magazine. His fourth novel, *Choke*, is being made into a movie. And I'm sure we'll see more.

And for these reasons, I keep the site going. In fact, I dare say the site is bigger, better, and more fulfilling for me than it has ever been.

For this reason, most days end the same. With the feeling that the Web site is out there . . . and that is good. As long as people have a place to come and discuss their favorite author, my job is far from over. It's been eight years in the making. We've gone from unofficial to official. We've now had more than six design overhauls. We've been on over eight servers. I've lost a staff and gained a family. But one thing remains constant, and that is Chuck Palahniuk and his ever-growing body of work. As long as he stays busy, so will I.